Contents

Preface

This Brief Workbook for Writers combines a very complete discussion of composition and grammar with a large number of exercises. Each element of writing receives succinct discussion at the beginning of the chapter. Following this discussion is a variety of exercises related to the material.

The strength of this workbook resides in the exercises, which in every case demand that the student demonstrate a thorough knowledge of the subject. The exercises related to composition foster the application of the writing principles presented in the chapter. For example, exercise materials related to the composing process in Chapter 3 encourage a student to react to a thesis and supporting statements by developing and supporting a counter statement (See Activity 3-2). In addition, the exercises related to grammar necessitate not only that the student be able to demonstrate a clear understanding of grammatical principles through the correction of errors but also that he be able to apply the principles in the combining and composing of sentences (See, for example, Activity 16-3 and 17-3).

The Brief Workbook for Writers is quite useful in itself as a succinct reference text and workbook. It is designed, however, to complement the Brief Handbook for Writers, and follows closely the organization and principles of the handbook. For this reason, the chapters of the _Brief Workbook for Writers_ correspond to those of the _Brief Handbook for Writers_

Even modest projects, such as this one, cannot come to fruition without the help of many people. For their unflagging support, we wish to acknowledge Prentice-Hall's acquisitions editor, Phil Miller, and our ever-vigilent, ever-helpful supplemental books editor, Gert Glassen. The quality of Prentice-Hall is clearly reflected in the excellence of its editors.

We wish especially to thank a genuinely supportive administration at Georgia Southwestern College and, in particular, James Russell, Arts and Sciences Division Chairman; Jerry Williams, Vice President for Academic Affairs; and William Capitan, President. We are fortunate to teach among students, colleagues, and administrators who value the profession of teaching.

Finally, we gratefully acknowledge Wilma Jones--frankly the most accurate and persevering typist who ever lived--and Betty Dumas, whose skill with the word processor is unsurpassed.

1 PLANNING

The writing process should begin well before one puts pen to paper. There are, in fact, several things which should precede the writing of a first draft. A successful writer should understand his assignment, whether this assignment is self imposed (i.e., a letter of apology, a job application), given by a teacher (i.e., an essay, term paper), or required by an employer (i.e., a business memorandum, report). A good writer must also consider the style and format most appropriate for the audience being addressed. The effective writer must also have adequate information--facts, examples, citations--with which to develop his writing.

1A CLARIFY YOUR PURPOSE FOR WRITING.

There are three major kinds of writing: informative, expressive, and persuasive. (See Ch. 2.) Each of these is appropriate to a different writing purpose and, in fact, can help to determine purpose. Ask yourself:

Am I writing to provide information to someone?
Am I writing to express my feelings?
Am I writing to persuade someone to accept a point of view?

1B GATHER INFORMATION.

After arriving at an understanding of purpose, begin to gather information related to the writing assignment. Sources of information include reading material, a wealth of which can be found in a library, and class discussions; however, these sources also include our observations, experiences, and imaginings.

You can obtain information from the library or from class materials by engaging in a process of investigation called <u>research</u>. However, you can obtain a great deal of material by engaging in an internal investigation called <u>brainstorming</u>.

BRAINSTORMING

Contemplate your subject.
Jot down in no particular order things related to your subject.
List concepts, examples, facts--whatever comes to mind.
Continue to write until you have listed everything you know related to the subject.

1C NARROW THE FOCUS AND DEVELOP A PRELIMINARY THESIS STATEMENT.

After gathering information, begin to consider the limits of the topic and begin to develop a thesis statement. A clear thesis statement narrows the focus of the writing, since it specifies certain limits to the topic.

Thesis statement:

Topic + limiting statement
(Student activity funds + should not be wasted on last year's films.

A good thesis statement avoids overly general topics, which could never be adequately discussed in an essay or research paper.

Too general: Love, Violence, Politics

Better topics: College Romances, Violence on the College Football Field, Student Conservatives

A good thesis statement limits a subject to some particular aspect which can be adequately developed in a paper.

Directionless: College romances are wonderful.
Violence on the football field is terrible.
Student conservatives are interesting.

Better: College romances often bring together quite different people.
Violence on the football field can sometimes carry over into other aspects of campus life.
Student conservatives are usually vocal on three issues: the economy, social reform, and world affairs.

A good thesis avoids stating the obvious, or repeating what is well-known or insignificant. In short, a good thesis statement passes the "so what" test. If, after reading a thesis statement, your response is "so what," the thesis statement is not an effective one. A good thesis provides an interesting and specific statement about a particular topic.

1D BEGIN TO ORGANIZE INFORMATION IN TERMS OF YOUR THESIS STATEMENT.

Brainstorming provides a wealth of material--some valuable, some worthless. It is necessary to sort through this material to determine if it relates to the preliminary thesis. Place a check beside those points or facts which seem to suit your purpose. Then, organize and supplement your brainstorming material. If there are facts or examples that seem to suggest an implicit point, then state that point. If, on the other hand, your brainstorming has uncovered good points which have little support, then provide facts or examples for support.

One form that this sorting and supplementing process may take is that of the preliminary outline. An outline is a kind of road map, guiding a writer through a maze of ideas. An outline provides a clear indication of the relation of certain facts to certain ideas and organizes the material in a way that allows a writer to plan the progress of the paper from one major point through the supporting material to another major point.

Preliminary Outline Format

Major Topic

I. Major point supporting the topic

Supporting facts and examples

II. Major point supporting the topic

Supporting facts and examples

III. Major point supporting the topic

Supporting facts and examples

Conclusion

If outlining proves ineffective, another way of sorting through the material provided by brainstorming is freewriting. This technique involves simply writing questions and statements related to the subject. The only rule of freewriting is that you continue the process until everything that needs to be down on paper is there. Freewriting is not as deliberate an attempt to clarify central points and to organize supporting material as is outlining. Nevertheless, freewriting often reveals a focus, a central point, or a pattern of writing which deserves development.

1E REVIEW THE PLANNING PROCESS.

1. Understand the nature of the writing assignment.
2. Clarify your purpose for writing.
3. Gather information.
   - Research material.
   - Brainstorm.
4. Narrow the focus of the material and develop a thesis.
5. Begin to organize and supplement information by means of a preliminary outline or freewriting activities.

Name______________________________ Date____________ Score__________

ACTIVITY 1-1, PLANNING

Listed below are a number of thesis statements. Some of these statements are satisfactory while others are not sufficiently limited or do not provide clear enough direction to be effective thesis statements. Place an X before those statements which would be ineffective. Be prepared to explain the reason for your choice.

1. College life is hectic.
2. Ethnic groups are increasing.
3. Gun control legislation could deprive citizens of certain constitutional rights.
4. The time normally wasted watching television could be more productively spent reading, exercising, or developing a hobby.
5. People are obsessed with food.
6. Young people are too apathetic and irresponsible.
7. The Hispanic culture holds certain values which could assist people from that culture in becoming good personnel managers.
8. Science is exciting and is rapidly developing.
9. Football has become a major source of funds and a major expense for colleges.
10. Most immigrants help the country.
11. The student alcoholic usually ends up failing in more ways than one.
12. Bad books should be censored.
13. Fraternities and sororities can provide important social support for the new student.
14. High schools are too easy.
15. Faddish diets are often expensive and unhealthy.
16. Pornography is a disgrace.

17. What can a person learn from getting married too young?

18. There are two kinds of beauty: a superficial physical beauty and an intrinsic moral beauty.

19. Minority groups have advanced.

20. History is a difficult subject which requires a particular knowledge of facts as well as an understanding of human character.

21. Living in New York provides cultural, educational, and professional opportunities which can be found in few other places.

22. A nuclear war would be devastating.

23. My best friend is truly humorous.

24. Most humor is based on incongruity.

25. Courage is a wonderful thing.

Name______________________________ Date______________ Score__________

ACTIVITY 1-2, PLANNING

For each of the following general topics, provide a clear thesis statement.

Example: Beauty pageants: *Although often criticized as sexist, beauty pageants can teach leadership and provide professional opportunities to contestants.*

1. College____

2. Morality____

3. Career goals____

4. Science courses____

5. Writing ability____

6. Immigrants____

7. Athletic scholarships____

8. Marriage____

9. Family____

10. Student Government____

11. Pornography____

____

12. Public Speaking____

____

13. Nutrition____

____

14. Nuclear Warfare____

____

15. Labor Unions____

____

Name______________________________ Date____________ Score__________

ACTIVITY 1-3, PLANNING

For each of the following thesis statements, provide facts or examples which support the thesis.

1. Athletic programs hurt the quality of a college's academic pursuits.

   A. ____

   B. ____

   C. ____

   D. ____

2. Athletic programs benefit a college's recruitment efforts in several ways.

   A. ____

   B. ____

   C. ____

   D. ____

3. A working mother who attends college on a part-time basis has several obligations which may take precedence over school.

   A. ____

   B. ____

   C. ____

   D. ____

4. There are clear advantages to growing up in a large city.

   A. ____

   B. ____

   C. ____

   D. ____

5. Smoking cigarettes is clearly unhealthy.

A. ______________________________

B. ______________________________

C. ______________________________

D. ______________________________

Name______________________________ Date______________ Score_________

ACTIVITY 1-4, PLANNING

Use the following space to practice freewriting. In your freewriting, either make use of the material gained from your brainstorming for Activity 1-1, or brainstorm and develop a thesis on a subject of your choice. The only rule is that you must continue writing until you have put all of your ideas on paper.

Name______________________________ Date______________ Score_________

ACTIVITY 1-5, PLANNING

Make use of the following space to brainstorm. Gather together ideas, facts, examples, etc. related either to one of the general subjects provided or to a subject provided by your teacher.

Suggested subjects:

The drinking age
Fraternities and Sororities
Terrorism

2 DRAFTING

Writing is a process involving a number of steps, each of which produces a further stage of refinement leading to a finished product. A draft is a preliminary version of a paper. It reflects an attempt, after planning activities are completed, to present the material in a form that is roughly equivalent to the finished product. This stage of the writing process involves drafting and revising the paper. A good paper may undergo several drafts and revisions before the paper is satisfactory.

2A CONSIDER CAREFULLY THE AIM OF YOUR WRITING.

If you are unclear as to the aim of your composition, your writing will probably reflect your uncertainty, and your reader, unfortunately, will share in your confusion. Determine the overall purpose of the writing, whether it is to inform, to persuade, or to express a certain attitude or feeling.

Informative writing provides the reader with an explanation regarding some event, theory, process, or the like. This writing does not provide an attitude about a subject but rather provides facts and information. In short, the aim is to clarify and inform the reader.

Persuasive, or argumentative, writing attempts to convince a reader to accept a certain viewpoint or belief regarding a subject--whether that subject is an occurrence, a situation, or a theory. In this writing, facts and examples are used not to clarify a subject, but to help convince the reader that your view regarding a subject is the best one.

Expressive writing offers insight into the writer's subjective response to a topic--the feelings, the emotions evoked by the experience. The aim of this writing is to share that personal experience with the reader.

2B REVIEW SOME OPTIONS FOR PRESENTATION THAT ARE USEFUL IN ACHIEVING YOUR PURPOSE.

Either the whole composition or parts of it may make use of certain techniques of presentation. Consider the various options when preparing to draft your paper.

Narration is a kind of writing that provides an account, a chronological report, of events or experiences.

Description is writing which provides a clear picture and often a striking impression of something or someone that has been observed.

Illustration is that kind of writing which explains or clarifies a subject or viewpoint by providing examples and details.

Classification is writing which seeks to group various subjects or parts of a subject and then to classify the subjects or parts according to a criterion.

Definition is writing that attempts to provide a precise meaning for a term or a concept. This kind of writing goes beyond a dictionary definition to offer discussion of distinguishing traits of the thing being defined and clear illustrations.

Comparison is a kind of writing which considers the similar and different features of two or more subjects.

Process Analysis is that writing which classifies and describes various steps or stages of an occurrence or procedure.

Causal Analysis is writing which clarifies the cause and effect relationship between events while considering the basis for the cause and/or the effect.

2C DEVELOP A SPECIFIC OUTLINE.

A good outline provides the paper with both a principle of organization and a clear direction. Writers who use good outlines usually compose unified, coherent papers.

An effective outline is one which presents a clear thesis and provides major and minor supporting points as well as some specific facts and examples.

Outline

Thesis statement: By the year 2010, the popular method of transportation may be very different from that of today.

I. Reasons for probable change

   A. Decreasing fuel supplies
      1. near depleted gasoline reserves
      2. unavailable alternate resources

   B. Rising transportation costs
      1. quadrupled gasoline prices
      2. higher vehicle ownership prices

   C. Increasing pollution problems
      1. harmful levels of combustion-related air pollution
         a. carbon monoxide
         b. airborne heavy metals
      2. growing levels of automobile-related noise pollution

II. Comparison of current and future methods of transportation

   A. Disadvantageous traits of the currently popular automobile
      1. inefficient fuel consumption
      2. expensive to own and operate
      3. pollution
         a. air
         b. noise

B. Advantageous traits of the future "high tech" trains
   1. extremely efficient fuel consumption
   2. relatively inexpensive as passenger transportation
   3. relatively non-polluting
      a. little exhaust pollution
      b. almost no noise pollution

Conclusion: Transportation will change considerably in the next twenty-five years.
   a. summary of reasons for change
   b. summary of changes
   c. closing points

2D WRITE A FIRST DRAFT OF THE PAPER.

A good paper will probably undergo a series of revisions. As a result, there are certain elements which should be focused on in this draft and certain elements which can be considered in later drafts.

Points to consider when producing a first draft:

1. Include a clear statement of thesis.
2. Concentrate on organization.
3. Provide a full expression of ideas.
4. Attempt to provide parallel phrasing among major sections of the paper.
5. Note places where additional examples or facts are needed.
6. Underline awkward wording and poor word choice for later revision.
7. Underline questionable spelling and grammar for later checking.

2E REVIEW THE DRAFTING PROCESS.

1. Consider the particular aim of your writing.
2. Consider kinds of writing useful for your presentation.
3. Develop an outline.
4. Write a first draft.

Name______________________________ Date_____________ Score__________

ACTIVITY 2-1, DRAFTING

Determine whether the following thesis statements are best suited to informative, persuasive, or expressive writing. Indicate your decision at the end of the sentence.

Example: High school students receive too little guidance when it comes to choosing programs of study. *persuasive*

1. An adult student has many obligations other than college. ________________
2. Before the end of the century, the cost of fuel and the increase in pollution will lead to the decline of the automobile.________________
3. Many people talk about a near death encounter, but few people have experienced one.________________
4. Most children would be more intelligent and well-rounded if they were not allowed to watch television.____________
5. Computerized dating services are useful for meeting people in a large city.________________
6. Americans place too much emphasis on physical appearance. ________________
7. There are several steps involved in cleaning a car's carburetor.________________
8. There are several types of magazines available for the avid reader.________________
9. One situation in my life probably gave me the greatest insight into human personality differences.______________
10. Travel to other countries can benefit a person both culturally and professionally.________________
11. A college student actually assumes several roles during a typical day.________________
12. After completing high school, one has several alternatives to entering college.________________

13. An economy car is superior to a luxury car in several ways.________________

14. My father's death was the one event in my life that greatly affected my maturity.________________

15. There are several groups of students that are generally annoying.________________

Name________________________ Date__________ Score________

ACTIVITY 2-2, DRAFTING

Develop a thesis statement on each of the following topics. Be certain that the thesis statement conforms to the purpose indicated.

Example: dating (persuasive): *Getting too involved at a young age can lead to social, psychological, and even financial problems.*

1. right to privacy (persuasive): ____________________

____

2. career opportunities (informative): ____________________

____

3. refugees (persuasive): ____________________

____

4. failure (expressive): ____________________

____

5. entertainment (informative): ____________________

____

6. death penalty (persuasive): ____________________

____

7. extracurricular activities (informative): ____________________

____

8. friendship (expressive): ____________________

____

9. teachers (persuasive): ____________________

____

10. transportation (informative): ____________________

____

11. the elderly (persuasive): ______________________________

____

12. growing old (expressive): ______________________________

____

13. humor (informative): ______________________________

____

14. professional boxing (persuasive): ______________________

____

15. written and spoken language (informative): ______________

____

Name____________________ Date__________ Score__________

ACTIVITY 2-3, DRAFTING

Identify each of the following passages in terms of the kind of writing it exhibits. Choose from the following: Narration, Description, Illustration, Classification, Definition, Comparison, Process Analysis, Causal Analysis.

Example: The events leading up to and including the Six-Day War are recorded for posterity. Months before the War there were marked differences between Israel and Egypt regarding boundaries. These differences soon led to military action. *Narration*

1. To understand many of the problems of the Middle East, one must understand Islamism. Islam is a religion which professes belief in one God and in Mohammed as God's major prophet.________________

2. Three major world religions have emerged from the Middle East: Judaism, Christianity, and Islamism. Each of these religions has distinct traits, and each of these major religions has a number of sects.________________

3. Although Christianity has its roots in Judaism and although Christ himself was of Jewish descent, the two religions have several striking differences.________________

4. I was awed by my first view of the ancient city of Jerusalem. The walls of the old city were made of stones piled twenty feet high, each stone now smooth from thousands of years of wear.________________

5. Warfare in the Middle East is all but hereditary. The predisposition to war is caused by the historical scarcity of natural resources. As a result of this scarcity, Middle Eastern peoples have always coveted the land which produces the resources.________________

6. The Jewish people have quite strict dietary laws. That is to say, orthodox Jewish people eat only those foods which are kosher. For example, they eat lamb or beef, not pork, provided that the lamb or beef is slaughtered and prepared according to Rabbinic law.________________

7. Since many of the Middle Eastern countries have no diplomatic ties, formal communications between these neighboring countries sometimes are rather complicated procedures. The first step usually involves identifying a neutral country and requesting that its leader or his appointee

act as a medium for communication. Next, the two countries present to him their views toward any problems as well as possible solutions. Then . . . ________________

8. Although relatively close in geographic terms, Tel Aviv and Tehran are ages apart in culture and outlook.

____

9. A hallmark of the Christian religion which emerged from ancient Jewish culture is the concept of sacrificial love. The love spoken of in the New Testament is quite the opposite of self-satisfying pleasure; it is, in fact, most properly charity.____________________

10. From an airplane at 3,000 feet, the Middle East hardly seemed attractive. The land was predominantly sand-colored and barren. Even while in the air, I could sense the heat and the dryness--I seemed to be able to taste the dust which whirled across the land below.

____

Name______________________________ Date____________ Score__________

ACTIVITY 2-4, DRAFTING

Presented below are the thesis statement and major points of an outline. Complete the outline by providing facts and examples to support the major points. Note "prompt words" in parentheses.

1. There are several ways in which a student can gain money to attend college.

    I. Students can receive funds from the college (What sources?).

    A.____

    ____

    B.____

    ____

    II. Students can borrow funds (What sources?).

    A.____

    ____

    B.____

    ____

    III. Students can work (Full time? Part-time? Where?).

    A.____

    ____

    B.____

    ____

2. In recent years, Americans have been increasingly interested in physical fitness.

    I. Much of what we read or see on television relates to physical fitness (Examples?).

    A.____

____

B. _______________

____

C. _______________

____

II. Youngsters are involved in physical fitness programs (Examples?).

A. _______________

____

B. _______________

____

C. _______________

III. Adults are revealing an overall concern with fitness (In which ways?).

A. _______________

____

B. _______________

____

C. _______________

____

3 REVISING AND EDITING

The term "revise" derives from the Latin revisere which means "to come to see again, to revisit." As the Latin root suggests, revision is much more than simply the correction of grammar and spelling. Revision involves a second encounter with your subject. It involves reconsidering the points which you make regarding the topic as well as considering any points not included in your paper. Revision demands that you see your topic again--reconsidering, adding, removing, and reorganizing. In short, revision is a major component of the writing process and involves intellectual and creative as well as editing skills.

3A REVISE EACH DRAFT OF YOUR PAPER.

Revision of a draft cannot occur immediately after the draft is written. At that point, you are likely to reread approvingly what you have written. It usually takes a day or so to become distanced from what you have written. At that point you are able to look at your material objectively.

There is more than one effective approach to revision. However, the following suggestions provide a guide to effective revision.

1. Question the aim of your writing. Is your intent clear from what you have written? Does your thesis statement provide the reader with an indication of the purpose and direction of the paper? Do the opinions, facts, and examples clearly support the aim of the paper?

2. Question the opinion of your writing. Play the devil's advocate and attempt to contradict the view presented in your paper. Can your thesis statement be strengthened? Can you offer better or more complete supporting material?

3. Consider the relationship of the thesis statement and the support material. Does the supporting material clearly relate to your thesis? Does the evidence suggest that your thesis statement should be altered? Does the overall discussion presented in your paper seem consistent and complete?

4. Consider the logic and unity of your paragraph. Does one point reasonably follow another? Does each paragraph seem to have a clear aim, and, if so, does it seem to accomplish its aim? Might someone have trouble understanding or following your points?

5. Check the point of view. Do you shift points of view? Does your attitude towards the topic seem to undergo an unwarranted change? Is your writing too formal, given your prospective audience?

6. Check the draft against your planning material. Is there material that resulted from brainstorming that should be included in your paper? Have you included all the material from your outline?

7. Review sentence structure. Is each sentence clear yet concise? Are related sentences clearly linked by effective transitions? Does each sentence follow the same subject-verb-object pattern, or does the composition contain a variety of sentence structures?

8. Review word choice. Are words used accurately? Does the paper contain inappropriate slang or colloquial terms? (See Ch. 40) Are there more exact terms than those used?

9. <u>Correct grammar and punctuation</u>. Is there a need to review a grammar rule before accepting a sentence as correct? Are commas, semicolons, and apostrophes correctly used?

10. <u>Correct spelling and capitalization</u>. Is there a need to check a spelling in the dictionary? Are -ed and -ing endings correct? Are proper nouns capitalized? Are some words capitalized unnecessarily?

Name________________________ Date____________ Score__________

ACTIVITY 3-1, REVISING AND EDITING

Revise the following thesis statements so that the aim is clear. If the thesis statement is adequate as is, place a C at the beginning of the sentence.

Example: Shouldn't everyone join a fraternity or sorority for social purposes?

A fraternity or sorority provides a person with social contacts and structured activities.

1. Athletics may or may not be harmful to a college's academic program.

____

____

2. Each year thousands of Americans die in automobile accidents.

____

____

3. Large cities have many sources of entertainment, and small towns can be quite charming.

____

____

4. Like many people, I listen to music and think some music may be good and some not so good.

____

____

5. People have many different views regarding whether the drinking age should be 18 or 21 years old.

____

____

6. Noise pollution can be physically and emotionally harmful and, as such, is a definite threat to the welfare of Americans.

____

____

7. Most people think that high schools should offer more basic courses and fewer electives.

____

____

8. A recent study suggests that smoking causes heart trouble as well as cancer.

____

____

9. In recent years, marriage partners have been pursuing independent professional careers. This phenomenon can be linked to an increase in divorces.

____

____

10. Billboards, billboards, billboards! All one sees along our highways are billboards.

____

____

Name________________________ Date__________ Score________

ACTIVITY 3-2, REVISING AND EDITING

Refute the material presented below by offering a contradictory thesis statement and supporting details.

Example: College is largely unnecessary to today's society. Most young people can obtain jobs without a college education. With the money provided by a job, a young person can get her own apartment and her own car.

Thesis: *College is essential in today's society.*

____

Support: A. *Most high technology positions require college level mathematics, science, and computer courses.*

B. *Many service oriented positions require advanced writing and communication skills.*

1. The American system of taxes is a burden which we should reject. Taxes take money from individuals while providing nothing in return. The federal government provides few essential services with our tax dollar.

Thesis:______________________________

____

Support: A.______________________________

____

B.______________________________

____

2. Eighteen is the proper age for one to drink legally. An eighteen year old is a responsible individual who knows when to drink and when not to. Most eighteen year olds are out to have a good time and would not harm anyone by drinking.

Thesis:______________________________

____

Support: A.____

____

B.____

____

3. It is clear that prayer should be barred from public meetings. Individuals should have a right to choose to be religious or non-religious. No person should be intimidated into praying when he might not want to.

Thesis:____

____

Support: A.____

____

B.____

____

4. The federal government should not limit the right of tobacco companies to advertise their product. Business should be free to persuade people to choose a particular brand. Cigarette smoking is a personal choice which does not affect anyone else.

Thesis:____

____

Support: A.____

____

B.____

____

5. Spanking is the best method of disciplining a child. Children, like other people, want to avoid pain and will act properly in order to do so. Spanking vents a parent's anger and lets the child know the difference between right and wrong.

Thesis: ____

____

Support: A. ____

____

B. ____

____

Name______________________________ Date_____________ Score_________

ACTIVITY 3-3, REVISING AND EDITING

Check each of the following passages to determine whether the writer remains consistent in his attitude toward his subject. If the viewpoint is inconsistent, revise the passage so that the viewpoint is consistent throughout.

1. America should not accept any more immigrants. This nation is a nation of immigrants, and most of our grandparents were immigrants. Immigrants are taking jobs from Americans. They usually accept those jobs which no American is willing to do. America is a great nation because of the variety of cultures provided by our ancestors, but the country doesn't need any more new ways of doing things.

____

____

____

____

____

____

____

____

2. Every state should have laws which protect motorcyclists. Each year hundreds of cyclists die from head injuries. These injuries could be prevented if helmets were made mandatory by law. Still, everyone should be free to do as he pleases, whatever a government tries to dictate.

____

____

____

____

____

____

3. Money is the root of all evil. The desire to obtain money leads to theft, to illegal drug sales, and even to murder. It is money which prompts greed, one of mankind's most destructive vices. Of course, money can also be used to accomplish good. Besides, it is not the money but the people who do wrong.

4. Capital punishment should be abolished. Our society is founded on Christian principles which affirm the spiritual dignity of each individual. To execute a person is to deprive that person of full spiritual development. Furthermore, capital punishment does not effectively deter others from engaging in crime. It is simply a primitive ritualized form of vengeance which accomplishes nothing positive. Only those people who harm helpless children and old people should be executed for the good of society.

5. Euthanasia is unethical and should never be legalized. No person or group of people should have the right to determine that an old person has outlived his usefulness to society and should be killed. In the hands of an unethical group, euthanasia could be used to exterminate racial minorities or people of the "wrong" religious or political persuasion. Nevertheless, doctors should take an active role in ending the endless suffering of the very ill, whether they are young or old. Then again, many newborn babies with major and expensive problems might be better off not having to live through all of the torment.

The grammar of a language is primarily the study of words and their function, especially in the written form. It also analyzes the basic facts of speech, explains the rules of usage, and interprets those established regulations governing the behavior of language.

4 PARTS OF SPEECH

The part of speech of any word is determined solely by the functioning of that word in a sentence. School grammars traditionally classify words into eight parts of speech: noun, pronoun, verb, adjective, adverb, conjunction, preposition, and interjection.

4A NOUN

A noun is the name of a person, place, or thing: boy, John, tree, maple, noise, attribute.

Nouns may be classified according to (1) form and (2) meaning.

Form

Simple nouns include all nouns which have not been formed by a combination of two separate words (girl, house, love, boat).

Compound nouns have been formed by combining words which have an individual meaning when used alone (bookshelf, sunlight, manpower).

Phrasal nouns are composed of words written separately or hyphenated (mother-in-law, Peter the Great, fountain pen).

Meaning

A common noun names a general class of objects (navy, instructor, student, jury).

A proper noun names a particular person, place, or thing (New York, Rin Tin Tin, John Doe).

A concrete noun names a physical and tangible object, person, place, or thing (table, blood, leaf, building).

An abstract noun names an intangible quality or condition or idea (beauty, love, determination).

A collective noun names persons, places, or things thought of as a group (crowd, audience, flock, majority).

A mass noun names a mass or bulk or quantity (wheat, corn, silver).

NOTE: With few exceptions, any word that can be modified by a, an, or the is a noun.

4B PRONOUNS

A pronoun, by definition, takes the place of a noun. Therefore, it usually has an antecedent, the word to which it refers. Pronouns may be classified by use according to the following categories: personal, relative, interrogative, indefinite, demonstrative, reciprocal, and intensive or reflexive.

Personal pronouns are comprised of first, second, and third person references:

I, me, mine, my	we, us, our, ours
you, your, yours	you, your, yours
he, him, she, her, it, its	They, them, their, theirs

I have told you that we should be served before they are.

The relative pronoun is used to introduce dependent clauses. It will have a function in the clauses as subject, object, or predicate nominative, and it will customarily have a stated antecedent (Who, which, what, whoever, whichever, whomever, whose, and sometimes as or but).

There is the man whom I told you about.
Give the book to whoever opens the door.
This is the house that Jack built.
Mrs. Jones is the woman whose house burned.
I have the same job as my mother had.

The interrogative pronoun is used to introduce a question, either direct or indirect (who, whom, whose, which, what).

What did you do for dinner?
Who is coming to the party
Do you know whose book this is?

The indefinite pronoun stands for some noun-word or phrase implied or understood but unspecified (few, some, any, much, none, nobody, everyone, something, etc.).

Many are called, but few answer.
Everybody has his work to do.
The candidate for office promises something for everyone.

The demonstrative pronouns (this, that, these, those) point out some definite person, place, or thing referred to.

This is my house, and those are the flowers I planted.

Reciprocal pronouns (each other and one another) are used to express mutual action by the persons or things indicated in the subject.

Yale and Princeton played each other for the championship.
Ah, love, let us be true to one another.

Reflexive and intensive pronouns traditionally include all of the -self pronouns.

The reflexive pronoun usually functions as an object or a predicate nominative. Its antecedent is usually the subject.

He torments himself by worrying. (object of the verb)
The children played by themselves in the nursery. (object of preposition)
The bride gave herself a new wardrobe. (indirect object)
Because of the lingering illness, he was not himself this morning. (predicate nominative)

The intensive pronoun is a -self pronoun which emphasizes or intensifies. It usually functions as an appositive.

He did all the work himself.

The teachers <u>themselves</u> were uncertain of the answer.

4C VERB

A verb is a part of speech which expresses action, being, or state of being. A <u>finite</u> verb is the verb within a clause which asserts or predicates. It is limited by both person and number. A <u>nonfinite</u> verb is not limited by person and number and does not stand alone as the verb within a clause. The three nonfinite verbs are gerund (a verbal noun with -<u>ing</u> ending); participle (a verbal adjective); and infinitive (the preposition <u>to</u> plus a verb form, used as noun, adjective, or adverb).

Verbs are classified according to meaning as <u>transitive</u> or <u>intransitive</u>. Transitive verbs are in either <u>active</u> or <u>passive</u> voice. Intransitive verbs have no voice and are either <u>linking</u> or <u>complete</u>.

Transitive active

The boy hit the ball. (The direct object, <u>ball</u>, receives the action of the verb.)

The woman was giving her husband a lecture. (The direct object, <u>lecture</u>, receives the action of the verb.)

Transitive passive

The ball was hit by the boy. (The subject, <u>ball</u>, receives the action of the verb.)

Her husband was given a lecture. (The subject, <u>husband</u>, receives the action of the verb.)

Intransitive linking

My teacher is a capable instructor. (The verb, <u>is</u>, links the subject and the predicate nominative.)

Roses smell sweet in the spring. (The verb, <u>smell</u>, links the subject and the predicate adjective.)

Intransitive complete

She smiled smugly at her audience. (There is nothing to receive the action of the verb; there are merely two modifiers.)

He came, he saw, he conquered.

Auxiliary verbs, commonly called helping verbs, help in the formation of tense, voice, mood, form, etc. Helping verbs include forms of the verb to be, to do, to have, and shall and will. Modal auxiliaries include may, can, might, could, would, should, ought, must.

4D ADJECTIVE

The adjective is a part of speech that modifies a noun or pronoun. Most adjectives may be classified as one of the following: articles; or demonstrative, numeral, indefinite, pronominal, or predicate adjectives. Adjectives that do not fit these categories are called descriptive (happy people, red hair, sour grapes, dishonest salesman).

Articles include a, an (indefinite), and the (definite).

The cat swallowed a goldfish.

A cat must have swallowed the goldfish.

Demonstrative adjectives (this, that, these, those) point out and modify nouns.

This lesson is assigned for tomorrow.
Have you contacted those potential donors?

Numeral adjectives indicate how many or in what order.

Thirteen football players were on the field.
I am the second of seven children.

Indefinite adjectives suggest an indefinite quantity or number (some, few, any, every, no, much, etc.).

Some students learned every rule in the book.
Much money has been squandered on a few students who show no interest in the program.

Pronominal adjectives are words normally used as pronouns but functioning as modifiers of nouns. They may be personal, relative, or interrogative (my, his, our, your, whatever, which, etc.).

My house is your house.
Which book has been selected?
Whatever treasure you find must be reported.

Predicate adjectives are subjective complements which follow linking or transitive passive verbs.

Her hair was blonde when she was young.
Why am I happy when you are sad?
The house was painted yellow at my request.

4E ADVERB

Adverbs are parts of speech which modify verbs, adjectives, and other adverbs. They usually answer the questions when, where, how, to what extent, and why. Thus they may be classified as adverbs of time, place, manner, degree, and cause. Not all adverbs, however, fit one of the categories. Some merely express affirmation or negation (yes and no, certainly, indeed) and probability or doubt (perhaps, maybe).

He often sings in the shower. (time)
He often sings loudly in the shower. (manner)
He sings here and there. (place)
I was very happy with his singing. (degree)
Wherefore art thou Romeo? (cause or reason)

Phrases and dependent clauses may also function as adverbs.

The derelict fell into the ditch.
He failed because he had no talent.

The -ly ending is only a superficial adverb ending. Some -ly words are adjectives.

He is a kindly father figure. (adjective)
She strongly recommended more discipline. (adverb)

Relative adverbs are often classified as subordinating conjunctions. However, they perform two functions: (1) modify verbs, adjectives, and adverbs; (2) introduce subordinate clauses. Some of the major relative adverbs are the following: as, after, than, when, where, whenever, whereby.

This is the place where I was born.
I went to law school after I had graduated.
She is as old as her husband.

I shall call you <u>when</u> dinner is ready.

4F CONJUNCTION

A conjunction is a word or word-equivalent used as a connective. It joins words, phrases, or clauses. The three major types of conjunctions according to function are coordinate, correlative, and subordinate.

<u>Coordinate</u> conjunctions (<u>and</u>, <u>but</u>, <u>or</u>, <u>nor</u>, <u>for</u>, <u>so</u>, <u>yet</u>) join items of equal rank: two or more nouns or pronouns, phrases, or clauses.

> Jack fell down <u>and</u> broke his crown, <u>and</u> Jill came tumbling after.
> I have never seen him, <u>nor</u> do I expect to meet him in the future.
> Your options are to marry her <u>or</u> to call off the wedding.

<u>Correlative</u> conjunctions are used in pairs to correlate words, phrases, or clauses: <u>neither/nor</u>, <u>either/or</u>, <u>both/and</u>, <u>not (only)/but (also)</u>, and sometimes <u>whether/or</u>. Correlative conjunctions must join similar grammatical constructions; otherwise nonparallel constructions will result.

> <u>Neither</u> the teacher <u>nor</u> his students had read the novel.
> He was <u>both</u> surprised <u>and</u> honored that he had been chosen.
> I have <u>not only</u> a wide library of books <u>but also</u> a good selection of magazines.

<u>Subordinate</u> conjunctions always join dependent and independent clauses. They do not modify anything within the sentence. Words usually functioning as subordinate conjunctions are <u>because</u>, <u>if</u>, <u>unless</u>, <u>since</u>, <u>though</u>, <u>although</u>, <u>provided that</u>. Some grammars include relative adverbs (<u>when</u>, <u>while</u>, <u>where</u>, <u>after</u>, <u>until</u>, etc.) as subordinate conjunctions, even though they also modify (See 4E).

> <u>If</u> he is guilty, he will be punished.
> Do not take the job <u>unless</u> you are willing to work.
> <u>Although</u> he is a church member, his opinions are not always orthodox.

4G PREPOSITION

The term "preposition" literally means the word "positioned before" a noun or pronoun which is called the object of the preposition. A preposition, in fact, always has an object, although the object does not necessarily follow the preposition. Common prepositions include the following:

after	but	from	to
at	down	until	with
before	out of	since	over
by	during	in	except
beneath	for	through	on

NOTE: Some words used as prepositions also can function as adverbs.

4H INTERJECTION

An interjection, from a Latin word meaning "to throw between," is a word or expression thrown into a sentence to suggest mild or strong emotion. It is not grammatically related to any other words in the sentence.

<u>Alas</u>! The game is lost.
<u>Oh</u>, for the glory of yesteryear.
<u>Hurrah</u>! The Falcons finally won a game.

Name_____________________________ Date_____________ Score_________

ACTIVITY 4-1, PARTS OF SPEECH

In the following sentences write n. above each noun and pro. above each pronoun.

1. This is the house that Jack built.
2. Is it true that the Empire State Building may be located in the state of New Jersey?
3. Whatever you want to do is fine with me.
4. A husband and wife should love each other more than they love themselves.
5. Who is the man I saw you with last evening?
6. A true artist is one whose work will last and who will be remembered.
7. Do you think that the majority of the students whom we teach will ever graduate?
8. This is the flock of wild birds that I told you about.
9. Love is one emotion which we cannot reasonably explore.
10. These are the times that try men's souls.
11. Everyone was startled by his remarks.
12. The soldier looked wearily at everything that lay at his feet.
13. Whoever looks for success usually finds it.
14. Four little mice ran across the floor, and everybody ran.
15. Perseverance is one key to accomplishing our goals.
16. Next year's calendar is one with new automobile pictures for every month.

17. If I can just complete one more lap, I will have run a mile.
18. Grandmothers are usually the first to give birthday presents.
19. Should the military be exempt from civilian laws?
20. The severity of an economic crisis can be measured by the severity of human misery.

Name______________________________ Date____________ Score__________

ACTIVITY 4-2. PARTS OF SPEECH

In the following sentences underline each adjective once and each adverb twice.

1. The robust man at the next table is not necessarily a glutton.
2. My first wife drove her car too recklessly.
3. A kindly old gentleman generously lent us his car.
4. I was not really aware that the energetic immigrants would be so industrious.
5. Perhaps the unusually gaudy outfit is characteristic of tourists.
6. The lovely old house where I was born has been destroyed.
7. Few people paint their houses purple unless they live in a very unusual neighborhood.
8. The most scholarly student often becomes a very good teacher.
9. Any child who looks unwashed should be sent home immediately.
10. I strongly recommend careful revision of this paper.
11. Usually, good friends are dependable in times of major crises.
12. The child was suspiciously quiet throughout the church service.
13. Many people become uncharacteristically hostile around income tax time.

14. Whatever she says, I strongly disagree with the callous practice of abandoning helpless animals.

15. He looked somewhat puzzled and very apprehensive.

16. Speak softly and infrequently, and you will be heard well.

17. Never buy a stiff fishing rod for rainbow trout fishing.

18. One careless move could easily result in a lifelong injury.

19. The noise was totally unbearable.

20. She had nearly completed the first assignment when she was given a second one.

Name______________________________ Date______________ Score_________

ACTIVITY 4-3, PARTS OF SPEECH

In the blank following each sentence, copy only the verb or verbs within each clause.

Example: Shall we dance?

shall dance

---

1. Do you know where the road to Xanadu lies?

---

2. I was looking for perfection until I met you.

---

3. Faulkner has been accused of writing Sanctuary as a potboiler.

---

4. Is it possible that a woman can become President?

---

5. Her greatest pleasure was sleeping on satin sheets.

---

6. The world will not long remember what we say here.

---

7. In the Middle Ages a ram was often given as a prize for wrestling.

---

8. Stop and identify yourself before you enter.

---

9. Is it reasonable to assume that we can have a rainy season in California?

---

10. What does he want us to do?

---

11. The unhealthy man was being given medication by an unskilled nurse.

---

12. The novel which I am now reading was supposedly written in twenty-four hours.

---

13. She has always been a better student than he.

---

14. I have not decided whether the student is deserving of the award.

---

15. My major interest has always been collecting lunar moths.

Name____________________ Date__________ Score__________

ACTIVITY 4-4, PARTS OF SPEECH

In the blank space rewrite the sentence, adding two prepositional phrases.

Example: He looked. *He looked at the small child in the park.*

1. I often walk.
2. I do not care.
3. Have you prepared?
4. The minister was convinced.
5. The rain falls.
6. The hot sun shines.
7. He wrote the book.
8. Jesus wept.
9. My feet ache.
10. Lovers believe.

Name______________________________ Date______________ Score_________

ACTIVITY 4-5, PARTS OF SPEECH

In the following sentences label each conjunction (conj.), preposition (prep.), and interjection (int.) above the word.

1. Ah, neither of you boys was present at reveille.
2. Both the mother hen and all her brood were pecking at the kernels of corn.
3. During the wintry blasts of December I always long for the warmth of July.
4. Everybody was present but John and his brother.
5. After dinner I did not know whether to take a nap or to read a book.
6. I knew him by reputation, yet I never met him nor heard him speak.
7. The rumors concerning his impeachment were neither confirmed nor denied.
8. Alas, the life of the athlete during the season is both tiring and demanding.
9. Since daybreak I have been working beneath the hot sun.
10. Do you know anyone who has written an essay this quarter?

Write five sentences using each of the pairs of correlative conjunctions.

11. (neither . . . nor)____

____

12. (either . . . or) ____________________

____

13. (both . . . and) ____________________

____

14. (not only . . . but also) ____________________

____

15. (whether . . . or) ____________________

____

5 SENTENCE ELEMENTS

The sentence is traditionally defined as a group of words having a subject and predicate and expressing a complete thought. The good writer will also have an understanding of other sentence elements such as objects, subjective complements, and phrases or clauses which modify.

5A SUBJECT

The subject of a sentence is either the person or thing that does the action conveyed in the verb or the recipient of the action (in a passive voice construction). The subject may be any noun or pronoun or substantive. The simple subject is one word (or a compound); the complete subject is the simple subject and all its modifiers.

Simple Subject

The leafy green <u>elm</u> is subject to disease.
My <u>mother</u> taught Latin for forty years.
<u>He</u> was questioned by the police and then released.
Basic to a good marriage is a good <u>income</u>.

Complete Subject

<u>Mary's keen interest in people</u> enhances her personality.
<u>A modest cottage covered in roses</u> was her dream house.
Was <u>the facade of the theater</u> attractive?

The subject of a sentence may also be a phrase or a clause.

Swimming in the nude is not a good winter sport.
That he was great is not to be disputed.
To be great is to be misunderstood.

A sentence with an imperative mood verb will have an understood subject, you.

Join the navy and see the world.
First turn the key in the ignition.

5B PREDICATE

The predicate is the verb within a clause. The simple predicate is the verb together with its auxiliaries; the complete predicate is the verb with all its modifiers and complements.

This medication makes me sleepy.

The subjective complement is used with an intransitive linking verb or with a verb in the passive voice. It may be a noun, pronoun, or adjective; it completes the predicate and refers to the subject.

My grandmother was an actress on Broadway.
I feel bad about your low grade.
Rest easy and stay quiet for a few days.
The walls were painted gray.
She was named head cheerleader her senior year.
It is I who am afraid.

5D PHRASE

A phrase is a group of words having no subject or predicate and usually acting as a single part of speech. Phrases may be classified according to structure as either prepositional or verbal (participial, gerundial, infinitive) or according to function as verb, noun, adjective, adverb.

My direction lay over the river and through the woods. (prepositional phrase used as adverb)
I am temporarily out of funds. (prepositional phrase used as adjective)
The woman wearing the blue dress is a beauty consultant. (restrictive participial phrase)

He wanted to win the series. (infinitive as direct object)
Listening carefully to a full orchestra is an impressive experience. (gerund phrase as subject)

Absolute phrases are grammatically independent of the rest of the sentence. They consist of a noun or pronoun with a modifying participle either stated or implied.

The party being over, we went home.
There being no further business, the meeting was adjourned.
The girls came up from the beach, their hair wild and unmanageable.

5E CLAUSE

A clause is a group of words having a subject and a predicate, usually stated, sometimes implied or understood. An independent clause may stand alone as a complete sentence; a dependent, or subordinate, clause must be attached to the main clause upon which it "depends."

Dependent clauses may be used as adjectives, adverbs, or nouns.

Simple Predicate

Michael Henchard was waving the flag vigorously.
The first lecture in the series will be given tomorrow.

Every clause, independent and dependent, will have a subject and predicate, even though in elliptical clauses they may be understood or omitted.

She is the girl whom I chose to marry.
While [I was] in the marines, I spent several years in the Orient. (elliptical adverb clause)

Any sentence may have a compound subject and/or a compound predicate.

Mary and her mother were late for the luncheon.
They ate a quick lunch and lounged by the pool.

5C COMPLEMENT

The complement is the word or words that complete the predication of the verb. The major complements include direct and indirect object, objective complement, and subjective complement, also called predicate nominative and predicate adjective. (See Verbs, 4C, for explanation.)

The direct object receives the action of a transitive verb.

Babe Ruth knocked the ball over the fence.
The psychic was giving a lecture on ESP.

The indirect object receives the action of a transitive verb and usually answers the question to whom or for whom.

My father bought me a car for graduation.
I found him a job in a department store.

The objective complement is a noun or an adjective which refers to or modifies the direct object and completes the action of the verb.

The owner painted the house white.
They named their first child Emily.
Do you consider me honest?

The adjective clause modifies nouns or pronouns or noun-equivalents. It may be either restrictive or nonrestrictive. It is usually introduced by a relative pronoun or a relative adverb.

The pastor is a man whom everyone trusts.
This is the book I purchased yesterday. (understood relative pronoun which or that)
She is one student whose scholarship is commendable.
Here is the house where I was born.
Fall is the season when the leaves change color.
Do you know the reason why you were called?

The adverb clause performs the function of an adverb to express time, place, manner, degree, condition, cause, purpose, concession, and result. It may be introduced by a relative adverb or a subordinating conjunction.

If I perform well in practice, I'll get to play on Saturday.
Unless you are prepared, do not come to class.
We lost the game because our quarterback was injured.
She is not so tall as I.

Noun clauses may be used in any way that a noun can be used: subject, object, subjective complement, appositive, adverbial objective, etc. A noun clause may be introduced by an expletive, interrogative pronoun, interrogative adjective, interrogative adverb.

That he was guilty as charged is still open to question.
I believe he is guilty. (direct object)
I was told that you had been given a raise. (retained object)
The question is whether you are ready to leave the hospital. (predicate nominative)
The fact that the humidity is high may indicate rain. (appositive)
I am aware that my payment is overdue. (adverbial objective)

Name________________________________ Date_______________ Score__________

ACTIVITY 5-1, SENTENCE ELEMENTS

In the following sentences underline each simple subject once and each simple predicate twice. A sentence may include more than one clause.

Example: *He scorched the toast.*

1. During the driving lesson the woman and her instructor were having nervous moments.
2. Did you consider calling off the wedding?
3. Basic to all your problems are a dominant mother and a passive father.
4. Neither of the boys plans to attend the ceremony.
5. I came to the university after I finished high school.
6. In the springtime the rose in my garden smells sweet.
7. To be great is to be misunderstood.
8. The mother, together with her children, was evicted from the apartment.
9. Each of the instructors must try to be prepared.
10. Let not your heart be troubled.
11. Some parents are too overbearing.
12. Michael, his friends, and my brother loafed around all day.
13. How interested are you in mathematics?
14. The third film in a series can often become boring.
15. Courage and valor remain important virtues.
16. Her purse and hat were left in the car.

17. Each of her children had filled out a library card and checked out a book.
18. Wishing for something doesn't make it happen.
19. Those who work will succeed.
20. Never speak to and never take rides from a stranger.

Name______________________________ Date_____________ Score_________

ACTIVITY 5-2, SENTENCE ELEMENTS

In the blank to the right, identify the underlined word(s) as one of the following: direct object, indirect object, objective complement, predicate nominative, predicate adjective. You may abbreviate.

1. I gave the dog a generous serving of meat. ______________________
2. They found the man dead of carbon monoxide poisoning. ______________________
3. My steak tastes better than your chicken. ______________________
4. She has been a dental hygienist for several years. ______________________
5. The midwife has been delivering babies for no payment. ______________________
6. Everyone knows that Jefferson Davis was named President of the Confederacy. ______________________
7. I feel awkward in your presence. ______________________
8. Mother gave me a BMW for graduation. ______________________
9. I shall make up the bed shortly. ______________________
10. Stay as beautiful as you are. ______________________
11. Let me be the speaker. ______________________
12. My father recently taught my younger sister how to drive. ______________________
13. Bill called my best friend a name. ______________________
14. Write your paper, and write it quickly. ______________________
15. Brenda saw Tom immediately after lunch. ______________________
16. I consider his actions childish. ______________________

17. A person's best friend is sometimes a good book. ______________________

18. Both the students and the teachers appreciated his comments. ______________________

19. The hurricane caused flooding throughout the state. ______________________

20. The hurricane caused wind damage on the coast. ______________________

Name________________________________ Date_____________ Score_________

ACTIVITY 5-3, SENTENCE ELEMENTS

In the blank to the right, identify the underlined phrases as absolute, gerundial, participial, infinitive, or prepositional.

1. Playing tennis in the summer is my favorite form of recreation. ________________________
2. The football player wearing the number 75 is a tackle. ________________________
3. The summer being over, we had to return to college. ________________________
4. The discussion concerning your future career is without direction. ________________________
5. The Cardinals want to win the World Series. ________________________
6. The fans left sadly, their team having been badly defeated. ________________________
7. I disagreed with his idea that attending class daily should be mandatory. ________________________
8. The inspector appeared without a warning from the company. ________________________
9. Hanging from the lowest branch, the sloth seemed at peace with the world. ________________________
10. I object to giving you advice about a personal problem. ________________________
11. The party being over, we left and did not return until the following afternoon. ________________________
12. By reading the stock quotations daily, he made a small fortune. ________________________
13. It is not always easy to choose the appropriate major in college. ________________________

14. The man having his picture taken is an old friend of mine from college. ____________________

15. To the victor belong the spoils. ____________________

Name______________________________ Date______________ Score_________

ACTIVITY 5-4, SENTENCE ELEMENTS

In the blank to the right, identify the underlined clauses as noun, adjective, or adverb.

1. Is this the class that you are having trouble with? ______________________
2. Why you are always complaining is beyond me. ______________________
3. Give the package to the lady who opens the door. ______________________
4. If you can keep your head in a crisis, you are indeed mature. ______________________
5. The place where I want to be buried is Tennessee. ______________________
6. Are you certain that the service has been discontinued? ______________________
7. I always knew the man I love would come along. ______________________
8. I always knew the man I love would come along. ______________________
9. The litigant was informed that his case would be heard in court. ______________________
10. This is the creed in which I believe. ______________________
11. I do not really know the person whom you are referring to. ______________________
12. What you have in mind for the Tobacco Festival does not seem altogether appropriate. ______________________
13. You cannot be a winner unless you are willing to demand the best of yourself. ______________________
14. Do you think the pattern I have chosen is too expensive? ______________________

15. I shall be in favcr of whatever you suggest. ______________________

16. You should always open your heart to the person who has the right key. ______________________

17. Are you happy that you have finally received your much deserved promotion? ______________________

18. Love is not love which alters when it alteration finds. ______________________

19. Yesterday is the time when you should have considered the man's proposal. ______________________

20. Do you know who is knocking at my chamber door? ______________________

6 SENTENCE TYPES

Sentences differ according to their purpose and structure. The purpose of a sentence may be to present a declarative, interrogative, imperative, or exclamatory statement. The structure of a sentence, on the other hand, may be simple, compound, complex, or compound-complex. The variety of purposes and structures provides the writer with an array of possibilities which he can employ in his composition.

6A BE FAMILIAR WITH SENTENCES THAT DIFFER ACCORDING TO PURPOSE.

Declarative sentences offer a statement regarding the subject. These sentence convey facts, examples, opinions and other information. These sentences end with a period.

I am weary of watching television.
She believes that the drinking age should be lowered.
My bedroom is being redecorated.

Interrogative sentences pose questions which make requests, seek information, or request affirmation. These sentences end with a question mark.

May I borrow your pencil?
How much did the dress cost?
Isn't this yours?
He passed, didn't he?

Imperative sentences state demands, commands, and requests. In most instances, the implied subject of the imperative sentence is the unexpressed subject, you.

Give the book to me.
Stand up, now!
Please have a slice of my cake.

Exclamatory statements express strong emotions, such as anger, surprise, and joy. These statements normally end with an exclamation point.

Get out of my life!
I can't believe it. I won $1,000,000!
I passed the test!

6B BE FAMILIAR WITH SENTENCES THAT DIFFER ACCORDING TO STRUCTURE.

A simple sentence has a single independent clause. This clause may or may not include adjectives, adverbs, and modifying phrases.

The man coughed.
Seated in the back of the church, the old man coughed throughout the sermon.
The young man and the old lady sat for hours and discussed world politics.

NOTE: As in the last example, a simple sentence may contain a compound subject and/or a compound verb.

A compound sentence has two or more independent clauses which may include modifying words and phrases.

She woke up very late; lying in bed, she suddenly remembered her appointment.
The walls need to be painted, and the roof needs repair.

A complex sentence has an independent clause and one or more dependent clauses.

When the auction was completed, the farmer's house, land, and equipment had been sold.
We left the game because our team was losing.
Hans, who speaks five languages, is a linguistics teacher.

A <u>compound-complex</u> sentence has two or more independent clauses and one or more dependent clauses.

> The women cried because they knew that many of their husbands would die, but the young children played as if nothing were wrong.

> If he is late one more day, I will give him a failing grade for the course, and I will remove his name from the roll.

Name______________________________ Date______________ Score_________

ACTIVITY 6-1, SENTENCE TYPES

Provide the correct end mark of punctuation in the sentences below, and identify the sentences in the blank to the right as declarative, interrogative, imperative, or exclamatory.

1. You remembered to close the window, didn't you ______________________
2. Help! We must escape the onslaught of the giant spiders ______________________
3. I did not know if you had changed your telephone number ______________________
4. President Roosevelt was elected for four terms as U.S. President ______________________
5. Forgive us our trespasses ______________________
6. Frailty, thy name is woman ______________________
7. Why we should have to go to convocation is beyond me ______________________
8. Why should I answer such a personal question ______________________
9. Let us all sing a hymn of thanksgiving ______________________
10. Odysseus arrived home in Ithaca after an absence of twenty years ______________________
11. Shut up ______________________
12. Please give so that the poor may eat ______________________
13. And what if I don't ______________________
14. I recently spoke to your uncle, and he intends to visit you soon ______________________
15. Whoever arrives late is usually the object of our gossip ______________________
16. Leave, and don't come back ______________________

17. How often does your sister visit ______________________

18. Whenever we try, we usually succeed ______________________

19. Can she help it if she is as beautiful as she is ______________________

20. Leave them alone and they will come home, dragging their tails behind them ______________________

Name________________________________ Date_______________ Score__________

ACTIVITY 6-2, SENTENCE TYPES

In the blank to the right, identify the following sentences as simple, compound, complex, or compound-complex.

1. The world will little note nor long remember what we say here, but it will never forget what they did here. _________________________

2. Going out for a long pass, the receiver turned awkwardly and twisted his ankle. _________________________

3. The football season really begins in September, but both coaches and players have been preparing throughout the summer. _________________________

4. Who is the man wearing the grey flannel suit? _________________________

5. During the rainy season nobody goes to the beach but the dedicated surfers. _________________________

6. While strolling through the park, I saw two ladies jogging. _________________________

7. The aphorism informs us that only a fool never changes his mind. _________________________

8. I never saw a purple cow, and I shall be happy if I never see one. _________________________

9. Both the man and his wife enjoyed their time spent in a variety of activities such as swimming, golfing, and fishing, not to mention admiring and spoiling their grandchildren. _________________________

10. There are several reasons why you should never try to go to college and work at the same time. _________________________

11. You may help with the cooking; then leave the serving to me. _________________________

12. After his ship comes in, I wonder if he will share his treasure with us. ____________________

13. The ballerina, though graceful, has not had enough experience to perform with our troupe. ____________________

14. I was born; I grew up; I devote myself to art, which I have always fancied. ____________________

15. Show me the evidence, for I am from Missouri.

Name________________________ Date__________ Score________

ACTIVITY 6-3, SENTENCE TYPES

Write sentences illustrating the purpose or structure called for.

1. an interrogative complex sentence

2. a declarative compound sentence

3. an imperative compound-complex sentence

4. an interrogative compound sentence

5. an exclamatory simple sentence

6. a compound sentence with a conjunctive adverb

7. a compound-complex sentence with a coordinate conjunction

8. a sentence introduced by an interrogative adjective

9. a complex sentence with a noun clause

10. a compound-complex sentence with an introductory adverbial clause

Name______________________ Date__________ Score________

ACTIVITY 6-4, SENTENCE TYPES

Add to the following groups of words to make the construction called for.

Example: in the green dress (simple sentence)

I have met the girl in the green dress.

1. the prophet warned (complex sentence)

2. after a night on the town (compound sentence)

3. the beige color on the walls (simple interrogative sentence)

4. my checkbook never balances (compound sentence)

5. walking through the forest (complex sentence)

6. be aware of the problem (imperative simple sentence)

7. defeated by a large margin (interrogative complex sentence)

____

____

8. while in the marines (compound-complex sentence)

____

____

9. decorating a large house (compound declarative sentence)

____

____

10. collecting antique glassware (compound-complex sentence)

____

____

7 SENTENCE FRAGMENTS

A sentence fragment is a part of a sentence, a "fragment," punctuated as if it were a complete sentence. A complete sentence has a subject and a verb, can stand alone as a statement or question, and sounds complete when read aloud. In contrast, a fragment may lack a subject and/or verb, or may seem to lack a sense of completeness when it is read aloud.

A fragment is corrected either by changing it so that it becomes a complete sentence or by joining it to a complete sentence.

7A KINDS OF SENTENCE FRAGMENTS

Certain clauses and phrases function as modifiers. As such, they must be in the same sentence as the word which they modify. A phrase or a dependent clause can never stand alone as a sentence.

Prepositional Phrase Fragments

He walked directly in front of a truck. Without even realizing it. (See Ch. 4.)

For the price of a plane ticket. She was able to spend a month in Italy with her friend's parents.

Along the sea coast right before sunset. There is usually a cool ocean breeze.

Revisions

He walked directly in front of a truck. He did not even realize it.

For the price of a plane ticket, she was able to spend a month in Italy with her friend's parents.

Along the sea coast right before sunset, there is usually a cool ocean breeze.

Verbal Phrase Fragments

Having waited an hour before boarding the bus. I was in no mood to stand up for the entire trip. (See Participle, Ch. 5.)

The ambassador was sent on an emergency trip to the Middle East. To negotiate the release of the hostages. (See Infinitive, Ch. 5.)

Their water and camping supplies running low. The mountaineers decided to return to their base camp. (See Absolute, Ch. 5.)

Revisions

Having waited an hour before boarding the bus, I was in no mood to stand for the entire trip.

The ambassador was sent on an emergency trip to the Middle East to negotiate the release of the hostages.

Their water and camping supplies running low, the mountaineers decided to return to their base camp.

Dependent Clause Fragments

Her grandmother gave her a box of old letters and pictures. Which she studied before writing her family's history. (See Adjective Clause, Ch. 5.)

After the young girl received news of the accident involving her sister. She wept uncontrollably. (See Adverb Clause, Ch. 5.)

Children do not always realize. That the easiest way to complete a task is not always the best way. (See Noun Clause, Ch. 5.)

Revisions

Her grandmother gave her a box of old letters and pictures which she studied before writing her family's history.

After the young girl received the news of the accident involving her sister, she wept uncontrollably.

Children do not always realize that the easiest way to complete a task is not always the best way.

Appositive Fragments

Most popular fiction readers are familiar with the novels of Robert Ludlum. One of the most widely read of the living mystery writers.

A land of green mountains, fertile plains, and uncrowded beaches. Georgia is the largest state east of the Mississippi River.

Not long ago my friends became obsessed with Trivial Pursuit. A game which requires that one know a great deal about very little.

Revisions

Most popular fiction readers are familiar with the novels of Robert Ludlum, one of the most widely read of the living mystery writers.

A land of green mountains, fertile plains, and uncrowded beaches, Georgia is the largest state east of the Mississippi River.

Not long ago my friends became obsessed with Trivial Pursuit, a game which requires that one know a great deal about very little.

Other Kinds of Fragments

The parents of Roberta Evans request your presence at her marriage. Would also appreciate your presence at the reception.

Most of us were amazed by the size of the comet. And frightened that it would veer from its course and crash into earth.

The students left their first class with a load of books. And enough homework to last for a week!

Revisions

The parents of Roberta Evans request your presence at her marriage. They would also appreciate your presence at the reception.

Most of us were amazed by the size of the comet and frightened that it would veer from its course and crash into earth.

The students left their first class with a load of books and enough homework to last for a week!

7B CONVENTIONAL AND ACCEPTABLE FRAGMENTS

Fragments are generally to be avoided in standard written English. They may be acceptable, however, in presenting rhetorical questions and responses, or in presenting familiar expressions. In some writing--usually impressionistic or fictional writing--fragments can be valuable devices for presenting dialogue, are suitable for providing emphasis, and are useful for describing a scene or establishing a tone.

Rhetorical Questions and Responses Using Fragments

Tolerate Terrorism? Certainly not.
Eradicate Terrorism? Probably not.

Familiar Expressions Using Fragments

So What?
All right!
So be it.
Goodness Gracious!

Dialogue Using Fragments

"Got the time?"
"What?"
"Time."
"Nearly five."
"Thanks."

Using Fragments for Emphasis and Tone

The sound of motors. Over Here! Bright search lights. Here! Here! The noise fades. The helicopter moves on. No hope now.

Name_______________________________ Date_____________ Score__________

ACTIVITY 7-1, SENTENCE FRAGMENTS

Identify each of the following word groups either as a sentence (S) or a fragment (F). Then, correct any fragment either by changing it into a complete sentence or, when possible, by joining the fragment to an adjacent sentence. Punctuate each new sentence correctly.

Examples:

__S__ A well-developed vocabulary is essential~~.~~,

__F__ ~~P~~p roviding students with verbal skills~~.~~ which enable them

__F__ ~~T~~t o communicate effectively and to comprehend what is presented.

__F__ A good vocabulary often ~~resulting~~ results in better grades~~.~~

__F__ ~~Thus~~ and overall success in college.

1. _____ There are several ways to develop a good vocabulary.

   _____ Without taking a special course or spending long hours of study.

2. _____ Often by paying attention to surrounding words.

   _____ Which may be synonyms or part of an appositive.

   _____ We better understand the meaning of the unknown word.

3. _____ A synonym is a word having the same meaning as another word.

   _____ A word that can be used as a substitute for another word.

4. _____ A word or word group renaming, identifying, or explaining another word.

   _____ Appositives often clearly define an unknown word.

5. ______ If the unknown word is followed by an example.

______ As is often the case.

______ The example can help to clarify its meaning.

6. ______ In addition, some understanding of the word may be gained if the sentence provides an antonym.

______ An antonym is a word which means the opposite of another word.

7. ______ Other methods failing to provide a clue to the meaning of the word.

______ The prefix of the word considered.

8. ______ Prefixes also provide some understanding of the word.

______ Prefixes such as pre or ante, which means before.

______ Or in, un, and non, which usually mean not.

9. ______ To look up each new word in a dictionary.

______ Perhaps is the best way to increase a vocabulary.

10. ______ However, before relying on the dictionary.

______ One should be aware of the kinds of information.

______ Which a dictionary can provide.

11. ______ Not only does a dictionary provide a word's definition.

______ It also provides its correct spelling, and its pronunciation.

______ As well as its etymology, its root or origin.

12. ______ A word's etymology provides insight into the meaning of a word.

______ And of other words that derive from the same root.

13. ______ The words amorous and amour, for example, are related.

______ Both derive from a Latin word.

______ From amare, which means to love.

14. ______ It is very important to make each new word part of your vocabulary.

______ So that it will be easily remembered.

______ To do this, the word's pronunciation.

15. ______ Once a person can pronounce a word.

______ And has used it several times in her conversation.

______ It is part of her vocabulary forever.

Name________________________________ Date______________ Score_________

ACTIVITY 7-2, SENTENCE FRAGMENTS

Correct the following paired word groups, eliminating any fragments. If the pair contains no fragments, write C, for correct, in the appropriate space next to the item number.

Example: _____ In recent years there has been a growing emphasis on study skills., Which are necessary skills if a student is to comprehend what he reads.

_____ 1. An important part of the study is retention. The remembering of study material over a period of time.

_____ 2. If one reads through school material one time with no further study. Approximately fifty percent of the material is forgotten within twenty-four hours.

_____ 3. There are, however, several study techniques. That can prevent the loss of information.

_____ 4. Probably the simplest one is the self-test method. It involves no training and does not take an inordinate amount of time.

_____ 5. It is a method which is most effective in dealing with large, fact-filled reading assignments. Such as those in history, psychology, sociology, or biology.

_____ 6. To practice this method most effectively. A student should first divide a long assignment into several sections.

_____ 7. Once a section is read. The student should then think of several significant questions about the major ideas contained in the section.

_____ 8. These questions should then be answered in the student's own words. Rather than in words remembered from the passage.

_____ 9. Expressing the ideas in his own words forces the student to assimilate the material. Thus insuring that he is not simply memorizing words that he does not really understand.

_____ 10. Once a student is able to express key points of a passage without relying solely on memory, he then moves on to the next passage. And begins the process again.

_____ 11. Research dealing with the effects of self-testing are quite conclusive. The student who practices this technique can retain almost all that he studies.

_____ 12. In fact, he may recall ninety percent of the material. For at least two to three weeks after he has studied it.

_____ 13. However, one aspect of this method is extremely important; the self-test must occur immediately after completing the passage. Not a day or even an hour later!

_____ 14. The student who waits a day before self-testing will retain only half of the material. When compared to the student who tests himself immediately after reading the assignment.

_____ 15. All things considered. Self-testing has proven to be easy to practice and very effective for learning new material.

Name________________________________ Date_____________ Score__________

ACTIVITY 7-3, SENTENCE FRAGMENTS

The following passages contain sentence fragments as well as complete sentences. Underline each sentence fragment. Then correct each fragment, rewriting it as a sentence, or linking it to an adjacent sentence.

Example: Proper study skills can make the difference. Between success and failure in college. Two important skills being proper listening and effective note-taking. Indispensable to every student's college career.

1. Students entering college often assume that everything they need to know is in their textbook. And that classroom lectures and discussion are sometimes interesting but mostly unimportant aspects of a course. Because certain knowledge and insights are only gained through classroom interchange. Students soon realize that success in college classes often depends on two skills. Those being proper listening and effective note-taking skills. Proper listening involves complete attentiveness to class lectures and active involvement in discussions. Also requires identifying key ideas and major issues. Important issues and ideas sometimes written on the board. Often signaled by an added emphasis in the teacher's speech or by an emphasis made through hand motions. The key points identified. The student then must make use of proper note-taking techniques. Effective note-taking involves copying down key points and related examples. Anything written on the board by the teacher. Any unknown word and, if provided,

its definition. And any "hard" fact. One involving numbers, statistics, or other data which support the main point. Notes need not be in sentence form. Phrases will do. They must, however, be organized. If not during class while they are written, then after class. Finally, it must be acknowledged. That notes are worthless unless they are reviewed. Ideally, twice--immediately after class, to organize the notes and learn the new material, and right before the next day's class, to review key ideas in preparation for new materials.

2. Time management is an important aspect of college life. That is not fully understood by the beginning student. Campus life includes an infinite number of time-consuming distractions. For example, activities in the student center, intramural sports, fraternity events, to name a few. The student who is going to remain in college. The student who learns to use his time most productively. The successful student will determine the best time to study. Which is that period of the day when the student is most alert. Too often, new students spend their midday hours socializing with friends. And spend their late night hours reading. Failing to realize that serious study is almost impossible if one is exhausted. Although there are some few exceptions. The students who survive in college are those who make studying a major activity of the day. Not a minor activity of the evening.

Name______________________________ Date____________ Score__________

ACTIVITY 7-4, SENTENCE FRAGMENTS

Correct the following fragments by incorporating them into a sentence which you construct.

Example: To insure that one's college career will be successful.

Revision

To insure that one's college career will be successful,

one must study diligently.

1. One technique for developing a large vocabulary.

____

____

2. Synonyms and appositives, which are often located near the unknown word.

____

____

____

3. Looking up the word and the pronunciation in a dictionary.

____

____

4. When a student learns to pronounce a word and to use it in conversation.

____

____

____

5. Although a person's vocabulary may be average.

____

____

6. That self-testing helps one to remember reading material.

____

____

7. Most of what we read forgotten the first day.

____

____

8. Time management being important in college.

____

____

9. To spend her best hours chatting in the student center.

____

____

10. Which is the time that a student should be sleeping, not studying.

____

____

____

8 COMMA SPLICES AND FUSED (RUN-ON) SENTENCES

Two major errors that one must avoid are the comma splice (or comma fault) and the fused (or run-on) sentence. The comma splice occurs when the writer uses a comma instead of a stronger mark of punctuation (semicolon or period) to separate two independent clauses not joined by a coordinating conjunction. The fused sentence occurs when independent clauses are run together with no punctuation at all.

COMMA SPLICES

Weather in the South is sometimes oppressive, the temperature often rises to one hundred degrees.

There are many items of interest at a garage sale, one may even find something of real value.

Unemployment is high in some areas of the country, one must always be prepared for the job market.

Revisions

Weather in the South is sometimes oppressive; the temperature often rises to one hundred degrees. (The comma splice has been eliminated by using the semi-colon correctly.)

There are many items of interest at a garage sale, and one may even find something of real value. (The comma splice has been eliminated by adding a coordinate conjunction.

Unemployment is high in some area of the country; therefore, one must always be prepared for the job market. (The comma splice has been eliminated by using a semicolon and a conjunctive adverb.)

FUSED SENTENCES

A college education is getting more expensive every year students must often find part-time jobs.

It is easy to do well in school just attend class regularly and study a few hours each day.

Revisions

A college education is getting more expensive every year; therefore, students must often find part-time jobs. (The fused sentence has been revised by adding a semicolon and a conjunctive adverb.)

Because a college education is getting more expensive every year, students must often find part-time jobs. (The fused sentence has been revised by making the first independent clause into an introductory adverbial clause.)

Name______________________________ Date______________ Score_________

ACTIVITY 8-1, COMMA SPLICES AND FUSED SENTENCES

In the blank to the left, write F (Fused sentence), CS (Comma splice), or C if the sentence is correct. Then correct the sentence by inserting appropriate punctuation.

______ 1. Composition is rarely a matter of luck, it is usually the result of proper planning.

______ 2. Although not all students write essays in high school, it is never too late to learn how.

______ 3. Most professional people spend a few hours each week writing, therefore, composition is a skill that should be learned.

______ 4. Clarity and conciseness are essential elements in writing it is necessary, therefore, to concentrate on these two elements.

______ 5. Correct spelling is also important after all, it makes written communication easier.

______ 6. Students who can spell correctly, however, are not always the best writers.

______ 7. A good composition always has worthwhile content there is no debate on that point.

______ 8. If you wish to write concisely, your rough draft should usually be longer than your final copy.

______ 9. Set aside a few hours each day for writing a short paragraph in a journal is good practice.

______ 10. Don't think of writing as a chore, consider it a pleasure instead.

Revise the following sentences to eliminate comma splices and fused sentences. Write C before any correct sentences.

11. Writing an essay is not always easy you must follow a few simple guidelines.

12. Start by thinking of something you are interested in, then begin the process by brainstorming.

13. Write down whatever comes to your mind you can always eliminate irrelevant ideas later.

14. Some teachers prefer essays written in third person, however, a narrative often uses first person.

15. Success in writing does not come from luck, it is the result of careful thought.

16. Many students rush into an essay without adequate planning the result is an undeveloped paper.

17. If students have a good background in grammar, it will help them write correctly.

18. Papers should be typed or written neatly in pen they should not be submitted in pencil.

19. Your instructor may ask for an impromptu essay, you should, therefore, be able to compose rapidly.

20. Nothing can be accomplished by procrastinating just do your best on each assignment.

Name______________________________ Date_____________ Score_________

ACTIVITY 8-2, COMMA SPLICES AND FUSED SENTENCES

Punctuate the following paragraph in order to eliminate comma splices and fused sentences. Add capitalization where necessary.

The introduction is an important part of the essay there are several things it should accomplish, primarily, it should gain the interest of the reader, this goal may be attained by shocking or surprising him. Sometimes a clever anecdote may be used, remember, though, that it must also be relevant. Often the good writer will begin with general but related statements, then he will narrow his topic down to a specific main idea this is what he intends to develop in the paper. The main idea is usually called the thesis statement it may also suggest a plan of treatment, this method is a safe one for the amateur writer, however, more accomplished writers often save their main idea for the conclusion. When the introduction is not well written, the rest of the essay may suffer.

Write five sentences, making use of the constructions and punctuation indicated.

1. (Independent clause + comma and coordinating conjunction + independent clause)

____

____

____

____

2. (Independent clause + semicolon + independent clause)

3. (Independent clause + semicolon and conjunctive adverb + independent clause)

4. (Dependent clause + comma + independent clause)

5. (Independent clause + semicolon and transition phrase + independent clause)

9 SUBJECT-VERB AGREEMENT

The basic rule to remember is that a verb agrees in number with its subject. A singular subject takes a singular verb. A plural subject takes a plural verb. Finding the subject, regardless of where it appears in the sentence, is the key to avoiding errors in agreement.

9A TWO OR MORE SUBJECTS JOINED BY AND TAKE A PLURAL VERB EXCEPT WHEN THE SUBJECTS ARE CONSIDERED ONE UNIT.

Biology and mathematics were his favorite subjects.
Gasoline and alcohol do not mix.
The secretary and treasurer was Amy. (The compound subject refers to one unit or person.)

9B WHEN SUBJECTS ARE JOINED BY OR, NOR, EITHER . . . OR, NEITHER . . . NOR, NOT . . . BUT, THE VERB AGREES WITH THE CLOSER SUBJECT.

Jack or Jill is coming down the hill.
Neither the teacher nor his students were prepared.
Either he or I have been defeated.
Not just the lawyer but the family members as well are required to attend.

9C A COLLECTIVE NOUN THAT INDICATES A GROUP ACTING AS A SINGLE UNIT TAKES A SINGULAR VERB. A COLLECTIVE NOUN THAT REFERS TO INDIVIDUALS WITHIN THE GROUP

TAKES A PLURAL VERB.

The choir is performing Handel's Messiah this Sunday. (A group acting as a single unit)
The choir are removing their robes before they go home. (Individuals within the group)

Words such as all, any, half, most, some take singular or plural verbs, depending on the reference. Often the object in the prepositional phrase following the subject will determine the number of subject and verb.

All of the pie was eaten.
All of the students were present.
Most of the money is still missing.
Most of the coins have been recovered.

Some nouns plural in form but singular in meaning take singular verbs.

Measles is a contagious childhood disease.
The local news appears on television daily.

9D SINGULAR PRONOUNS REQUIRE SINGULAR VERBS. The following pronouns are singular: anyone, anybody, someone, somebody, everyone, everybody, either, neither, each, anything.

Either of the girls is a good candidate.
Everybody has thrown his hat into the ring.
Almost nobody is immune to flattery.

9E THE NUMBER OF A RELATIVE PRONOUN AND ITS VERB IS DETERMINED BY THE PRONOUN'S ANTECEDENT.

The students who study hard are few.
The changes in the curriculum which are significant are noted below.
The antecedents that govern relative pronouns are usually stated.
She is one of those girls who are always tardy.

9F PHRASES SUCH AS TOGETHER WITH, AS WELL AS, AND IN ADDITION TO DO NOT AFFECT THE NUMBER OF THE VERB.

The mother together with her five children is staying at home.
Our one friend, as well as our enemies, was in trouble.

9G A NUMBER IS USUALLY PLURAL WHEN IT MEANS MANY. THE NUMBER IS USUALLY SINGULAR.

A number of football players were injured.
The number of injured players is increasing.
A number on the jersey is essential for identification.

9H THE VERB AGREES WITH ITS SUBJECT, NOT WITH ITS PREDICATE NOMINATIVE.

The only important item in the room was the paintings.
The main thing to see is the weeping willows.

9I THE ADVERB HERE OR THERE OR THE EXPLETIVE THERE AT THE BEGINNING OF A SENTENCE DOES NOT GOVERN THE NUMBER OF THE VERB.

There but for the grace of God go I.
There are a dog, a cat, and a canary in my house.

9J CHECK THE DICTIONARY FOR THE SINGULAR AND PLURAL FORMS OF FOREIGN NOUNS.

The phenomena in the heavens are remarkable.
The alumna has been accepted as our counselor.

Name____________________ Date__________ Score________

ACTIVITY 9-1, SUBJECT-VERB AGREEMENT

Underline the correct verb within parentheses. In the blank to the left write the subject of that verb. Copy both parts of any compound subject.

Example: *James Joyce - Homer* James Joyce and Homer (has written, have written) of Ulysses.

____________________ 1. Neither The Prince nor The Reivers (is, are) in my personal library.

____________________ 2. Standing on the lower shelf (is, are) The Deerslayer and other works by Cooper.

____________________ 3. Both Harper Lee and Margaret Mitchell (has, have) given us one successful novel.

____________________ 4. The novel, as well as collections of short stories, (has, have) been attempted by many writers.

____________________ 5. Grace Metalious is another of those novelists who (has, have) made a reputation on one book.

____________________ 6. The teacher said that either The Frogs or The Birds (is, are) worthwhile reading.

____________________ 7. The criterion which (motivates, motivate) many writers (is, are) financial success.

____________________ 8. Politics (plays, play) a major role in A Tale of Two Cities.

____________________ 9. It is neither my roommate nor I who (is, am, are) reading the works of Willa Cather.

____________________ 10. Neither of King Lear's two oldest daughters (shows, show) much affection.

Underline the correct word within parentheses.

11. A summer vacation in wilderness areas (comes, come) close to perfection.

12. Neither the heat nor the mosquitoes (seems, seem) to matter to the outdoorsman.

13. The croaking of the frogs, together with the sounds of other animals, (is, are) native to the Everglades.

14. One must decide carefully the points of interest which he thinks (is, are) worth visiting.

15. In Florida there (is, are) the sound of the beckoning surf and the shimmering white sand.

16. (Is, Are) either of you taking a vacation?

17. Many a person (has, have) never been able to afford a Caribbean cruise.

18. On my last vacation my driver and financial supporter (was, were) my older brother.

19. Neither he nor I (is, am, are) planning to stay for more than a week.

20. He is one of those people who always (returns, return) from vacation tired and peevish.

Name______________________________ Date______________ Score_________

ACTIVITY 9-2, SUBJECT-VERB AGREEMENT

Make sentences using the following nouns as subjects. Check your dictionary to determine their number.

1. phenomena____

____

2. criterion____

____

3. media____

____

4. curriculum____

____

5. alumna____

____

6. alumni____

____

7. data____

____

8. synopses____

____

9. stratum____

____

10. phyla____

____

11. crises____

____

12. vertebrae_____________________________________

____

13. genera____

____

14. stylus____

____

15. ganglia_______________________________________

____

Name_____________________________ Date_____________ Score________

ACTIVITY 9-3, SUBJECT-VERB AGREEMENT

Correct any errors in agreement of subject and verb by crossing out any incorrect verb and writing the correct form above it. Write C beside any correct sentence.

1. John's keen awareness of people and places make him a good conversationalist.
2. Almost everyone in the biology classes, even the mature students, are having trouble dissecting the frogs.
3. Both the administrators and the faculty are making many changes in the curriculum which, according to our research, is going to improve the quality of education.
4. The news on radio and television tell us that measles are a problem on the college campus.
5. Is it true that the criteria for selection of the officers was questioned?
6. The number of students who seek government loans seems to be increasing.
7. If every one of us who apply decide to attend, we ought to have a large class.
8. When the alumnae return to the school, they will find significant changes.
9. Neither the students nor their professor seem to believe in regular class attendance.
10. What do you think of the data which has been collected by the research assistant?

11. Are either of you able to provide financial assistance to the needy?
12. The mother goose, together with her five goslings, swims across the lake each afternoon.
13. The exterior of the old houses and theaters were no longer attractive.
14. Tim is one of the few football players who have made both the team and the honor roll.
15. So far as finding anyone in the deserted villages and towns were concerned, we had given up hope.
16. It is the informal dress of the students and teachers which concern us.
17. Here and there in the old cave was a hanging bat, stalagmites, and an occasional skull.
18. Neither my roommate nor I enjoys being deprived of an allowance.
19. There were no electricity and no indoor plumbing in any of the houses.
20. She lived in one of those Victorian houses that fronts on Lee Street and is distinguished by a large porch.

Name______________________________ Date______________ Score_________

ACTIVITY 9-4, SUBJECT-VERB AGREEMENT

In the following sentences, underline the correct form within parentheses, and be prepared to justify your choice.

1. She is the only one of the cheerleaders who (was, were) late for practice.

2. Cheerleading, as well as playing baseball and other sports, (requires, require) talent and dedication.

3. There (is, are) a tackle, a guard, and a quarterback in the locker room.

4. Almost every branch of the Armed Services (asks, ask) that the members be physically fit.

5. The audience at sports presentations often (shifts, shift) restlessly in their seats.

6. The media (presents, present) items about athletes on a daily basis.

7. Neither he nor I (is, am, are) able to understand that the news about athletic events (does, do) not appeal to everyone.

8. The phenomenon of male homecoming queens (is, are) limited to only a few schools.

9. He is one of those football players who always (demands, demand) public attention.

10. (Does, do) either of you agree that ten dollars (is, are) too much to pay for a ticket?

11. Each year the cheerleading squad (is, are) assigned individual rooms in the dormitory.

12. Common sense, as well as economics, (tells, tell) us that athletes often play because of the scholarship.

13. Georgia is one of the teams in the Southeastern Conference that usually (posts, post) a winning season.

14. Athletics (is, are) not for everyone, but the number of people who choose to participate (is, are) growing annually.

15. The main reason why some teenage girls like football (is, are) the players.

16. One of the major problems with college athletics (seems, seem) to be rowdy spectators.

17. Only one spectator out of ten (is, are) there to watch the game.

18. A large number (comes, come) to the game simply to socialize, yell, and disturb others.

19. Violence in athletic contests unfortunately (has, have) moved from the playing field to the stands.

20. Careful planning, as well as clear policies and stiff penalties, (provides, provide) the best solution to this growing problem.

10 PRONOUN CASE, AGREEMENT, AND REFERENCE

Pronoun case is determined by the use of the pronoun in the sentence (as subject, object, predicate nominative, etc.). The three cases in English are subjective (or nominative), objective, and possessive.

10A USE THE SUBJECTIVE (NOMINATIVE) CASE OF THE PRONOUN (I, YOU, HE, SHE, IT, WE, YOU, THEY, WHO, WHOEVER) FOR THE FOLLOWING: SUBJECT OF A VERB, SUBJECTIVE COMPLEMENT, APPOSITIVE.

He and I are taking flying lessons. (subject of the verb are taking)
It is I who called you. (I is the subjective complement; who is subject of the verb called.)
The two best candidates, Sherry and I, were elected with little opposition. (I is in apposition with the subject, candidates.)
She is not so tall as he. (subject of the elliptical clause he is)
Give the medal to whoever wins the race. (Subject of the verb wins)

10B USE THE OBJECTIVE CASE OF THE PRONOUN (ME, YOU, HIM, HER, IT, US, THEM, WHOM, WHOMEVER) FOR THE FOLLOWING: DIRECT OR INDIRECT OBJECT OF A VERB, VERBAL, OR PREPOSITION; APPOSITIVE; SUBJECT OF AN INFINITIVE.

The teacher punished us for being tardy. (direct object of verb punished)
The company offered him a large pension. (indirect object of verb offered)
Giving him and her a job was a mistake. (compound indirect object of a verbal)
This information is just for you and me. (compound object of preposition for)
The awards were given to the top students, him and her. (in apposition to the object students)
I wanted him to mow the lawn. (subject of the infinitive to mow)

10C THE INFINITIVE TO BE IS SOMEWHAT TROUBLESOME, BUT THE RULES THAT GOVERN IT ARE SIMPLE. The subject of the infinitive to be is in the objective case. (I expected him to be happy.) If the subject and the subjective complement of to be are expressed, both are in the objective case. (I want my wife to be her. I want her to be my wife.) If only the subjective complement of to be is expressed, it will be in the subjective (nominative) case. (After reading about Cinderella, I wanted to be she in the school play.)

10D USE THE POSSESSIVE CASE BEFORE A GERUND.

His singing in the shower is unpleasant.
We questioned her attending a large university.

10E USE THE COMPOUND PERSONAL PRONOUNS (MYSELF, HERSELF, THEMSELVES, ETC.) ONLY AS INTENSIVE OR REFLEXIVE PRONOUNS.

She tied the bandage herself. (intensive)
She cut herself while tying the bandage. (reflexive)

AGREEMENT OF PRONOUN AND ANTECEDENT

A pronoun agrees with its antecedent in number, gender, and person.

10F IN FORMAL USAGE THE WORDS ANYONE, ANYBODY, EACH, EITHER, EVERYBODY, NEITHER, NOBODY, AND SOMEBODY ARE SINGULAR AND WHEN USED AS ANTECEDENTS REQUIRE A SINGULAR PRONOUN.

Everybody who wants to be exempt should raise his

hand.
Each of the girls was required to do her own laundry.
Neither of the students has turned in his homework.

NOTE: Avoid sexist use of the third person masculine pronoun if it is offensive to your audience. Instead of writing: Each candidate must be willing to do his best, you may write: All candidates must be willing to do their best.

10G A PRONOUN MUST AGREE WITH THE NEARER OF TWO ANTECEDENTS JOINED BY OR OR NOR.

Neither the azalea nor the camellias have lost their leaves.
We could not determine whether the administrator or the faculty members were remiss in their duties.

10H AS A GENERAL RULE, USE WHO TO REFER TO PERSONS, WHICH TO REFER TO THINGS, AND THAT TO REFER TO PERSONS OR THINGS.

The boy who won the spelling bee is in the eighth grade.
This door, which is almost off its hinges, should be repaired.
The man, the house, and the dog that appear in the picture are realistically presented.

PRONOUN REFERENCE

10I AVOID VAGUE OR UNCLEAR PRONOUN REFERENCE. THE ANTECEDENT SHOULD BE EXPRESSED, NOT IMPLIED, OR THE SENTENCE SHOULD BE REVISED ALTOGETHER.

Vague: I wanted to be a doctor because it is a good profession.
Improved: I wanted to major in medicine because it is a good profession.

Vague: My car has not been running well, which is why I have not visited you recently.
Vague: My car has not been running well. That is why I have not visited you recently.
Improved: Because my car has not been running well, I have not visited you recently.

Vague: Although the applicants were nervous, they tried not to show it.

Improved:	The applicants tried not to show that they were nervous.
Vague:	The father told his son that <u>he</u> needed a new car.
Improved:	The father needed a new car, and his son told him so.
Improved:	The father told his son, "You need a new car."

Name____________________ Date__________ Score________

ACTIVITY 10-1, PRONOUN CASE, AGREEMENT, AND REFERENCE

Revise the following sentences to eliminate vague or unclear pronoun reference. If a sentence is correct, write C before it.

1. Life in the dormitory is exciting, which is the main reason I have chosen to live there.

____

____

2. One gets to meet new friends in a campus dormitory. That is a good reason to live there.

____

____

3. Most dormitories are nicely heated and air-conditioned, which makes life there comfortable.

____

____

4. The person who lives on campus may tell his roommate that he needs to clean the room.

____

____

5. They say that commuting to college is very expensive.

____

____

6. My roommate is very intelligent, but his grades don't always show it.

____

____

7. In my freshman year I had to learn to get along with a sloppy roommate. That was not easy for me.

8. If you commute to college every day, it can get expensive.

9. On the way to school today I bought gasoline, which cost me several dollars.

10. If roommates could respect each other's privacy, it would make dormitory life more pleasant.

Name______________________________ Date_______________ Score________

ACTIVITY 10-2, PRONOUN CASE, AGREEMENT, AND REFERENCE

Underline the correct word within parentheses.

1. Ultimately every man must be responsible for (his, their) own success or failure.

2. The alumna of a good college (is, are) often successful in (his, her, their) chosen profession.

3. Neither the local high school nor the larger colleges and universities can guarantee that (its, their) graduates will succeed.

4. A large corporation makes its employees happy if (it offers, they offer) them annual bonuses.

5. It is either the person who works diligently or those who contribute new ideas that (is, are) most appreciated by (his, their) employer.

6. Each of the men who (graduates, graduate) from our business college will find (himself, themselves, theirselves) a job this year.

7. Not everyone in our graduating class can treat (himself, themselves) to a new car immediately.

8. If a newlywed couple (is, are) working, (it, they) can achieve financial security.

9. A woman with a liberal arts degree or one with a business degree should choose (her, their) first job carefully.

10. Nobody but a mother and father (is, are) able to appreciate the value of an education to (his, her, their) own child.

11. It is necessary for you and (I, me) to make a good impression in an interview.

12. Let us discuss, then, you and (I, me), how we shall respond to the questions.

13. The interviewer gave John and (I, me, myself) an opportunity to join (he, him) and his staff for dinner.

14. Punctuality was important in getting (he and I, him and me) a job.

15. Nobody was present at the interview except another applicant and (I, me, myself).

16. The applicant (who, whom) the company seemed most interested in sat beside John and (I, me) in the outer office.

17. He doubted (me, my) being properly dressed for the interview.

18. The corporation will give the job to (whoever, whomever) seems most qualified.

19. I answered that it was my brother and (I, me) (who, whom) the company had first contacted.

20. Apparently the office manager wanted the new employee to be (I, me).

Name______________________________ Date______________ Score__________

ACTIVITY 10-3, PRONOUN CASE, AGREEMENT, AND REFERENCE

The following sentences may contain errors in pronoun reference, case, or agreement. Correct any errors you find. If there are no errors, write C beside the sentence.

1. We painted the dormitory room bright blue, but it didn't improve the study habits of whomever lived in it.
2. The company is always telling their employees that they must increase sales.
3. Whom shall I say is calling?
4. It is necessary for you and I to cut down on expenses.
5. Can you recommend John and I as people who you can trust?
6. Because the rear window was covered with books and clothing, it prevented me seeing the traffic behind me.
7. During the day each of us will encounter people who we must deal with.
8. Although the teacher who I liked best was well educated, he did not always show it.
9. Not one of my colleagues has made any changes in their resumé.
10. There are many students besides Martin and I who you might consider worthy of the scholarship.
11. The teacher wanted to know whether either of the dogs who had followed John and I to school had been given their daily meal.

12. Everyone in their right mind must know that each of us must be responsible for their own failure.

13. Whom do you consider, John or I, to be the best writer in the freshman class?

14. I do not know who to invite to the party.

15. We decided to change the carpet in our guest room, which had been suggested by someone whom Mother and myself could trust.

16. Either the teacher or the lab assistant has invited Sherry and I to come by for extra help when they are not in class.

17. Let Ellen and I know who you think would be acceptable to the sorority members.

18. Select whoever you want; just between you and I, the whole affair is ludicrous.

19. I shall sell my collection to she or you, whomever will pay the full price.

20. For some reason I took Mr. Mathews to be him.

Name________________________ Date____________ Score________

ACTIVITY 10-4, PRONOUN CASE, AGREEMENT AND REFERENCE

Underline the proper case form of the pronoun within parentheses.

1. Just between you and (I, me), the gardening is too demanding for (she, her) and her husband.
2. We did not know (who, whom) to invite to the party.
3. My sister has always been smarter than (I, me).
4. No students but John and (I, me) have earned a scholarship for next year.
5. It is (I, me) (who, whom) you must answer to.
6. What is the reason for (me, my) having to study foreign languages?
7. I assume that the new chairman will be (he, him).
8. I want the new chairman to be (he, him).
9. The professor asked John and (I, me) to leave the classroom.
10. Our employer gave Mary and (I, me) an hour to clear our desks.
11. Give your charity to (whoever, whomever) you think deserves it most.
12. You will share the room with (whoever, whomever) you are assigned for the quarter.
13. Nobody but the winners--John, Mary, and (I, me)--will participate in the next track meet.
14. She is not so tall as (he, him), but she is the same height as (I, me).
15. Our speech teacher wants Wilma and (I, me) to be on the debate team.

11 VERB FORMS

Each verb has four forms: present, past, past participle, and present participle. A good dictionary provides the forms for each verb.

Present	Past	Past Participle	Present Participle
begin	began	begun	beginning
drink	drank	drunk	drinking
freeze	froze	frozen	freezing
go	went	gone	going
lay	laid	laid	laying
lie	lay	lain	lying
swim	swam	swum	swimming

The past participle form is generally used after being and for all perfect tenses (those tenses using has, have, or had). The present participle is generally used for progressive forms (those -ing forms using am, is, are, was, were, been). (See also participle and gerund phrases, Ch. 5.)

11A AVOID NON-STANDARD, SLANG, OR INVENTED VERB FORMS.

Non-Standard form

We had swam until we were exhausted.

Revision

We had swum until we were exhausted.

Slang form

We were mostly rapping about our summer vacation.

Revision

We mostly were discussing our summer vacation.

Invented form

She has broked Mother's favorite vase.

Revision

She has broken Mother's favorite vase.

11B AVOID MISUSE OF LIE/LAY AND SIT/SET.

To lie (lie, lay, lain, lying) means "to rest or recline." To lay (lay, laid, laid, laying) means "to put or place" something. To sit (sit, sat, sat, sitting) means "to be seated." To set (set, set, set, setting) means to "to place" somewhere.

He lies in bed. Yesterday, he lay in bed.

She lays the book on the table. Yesterday, she laid it there.

She sits uncomfortably for hours. Then she walks about her house setting potpourri upon her mantels.

The old man had ~~set~~ down his heavy load and was sitting upon the side of the road.

Name____________________________ Date__________ Score__________

ACTIVITY 11-1, VERB FORMS

Make use of a dictionary, if necessary, to identify the past, past participle, and present participle of each of the following verbs. List each form in the appropriate place.

PRESENT	PAST	PAST PARTICIPLE	PRESENT PARTICIPLE
awake			
break			
bring			
buy			
cancel			
choose			
do			
drown			
fly			
get			
give			
grow			
keep			
know			
lead			
leave			
lend			
let			
make			

PRESENT	PAST	PAST PARTICIPLE	PRESENT PARTICIPLE
pass	________	________	________
prove	________	________	________
raise	________	________	________
rise	________	________	________
seek	________	________	________
speak	________	________	________
steal	________	________	________
take	________	________	________
tear	________	________	________
think	________	________	________
write	________	________	________

Name______________________________ Date____________ Score__________

ACTIVITY 11-2, VERB FORMS

Underline the correct verb form.

1. A stack of papers was (lying, laying) on the desk.
2. The opportunity of a lifetime (lay, laid) before me.
3. Has the book (lay, lain) on the ground very long?
4. She (was sitting, was setting) forth a proposal regarding school policies.
5. The trapper (set, setted) his snares among the brush.
6. If a tool (lies, lays) unused, it will rust.
7. Before we arrived, they (had sat, had set) additional china and silverware.
8. He (had lain, had laid) unconscious an hour before he awoke.
9. The movie had the audience (sitting, setting) on the edge of their seats.
10. Our departed grandfather (lies, lays) peacefully in a rural cemetery.
11. Please (lie, lay) the pen on my desk.
12. I am afraid that I have (mislain, mislaid) my checkbook.
13. Had he (lain, laid) the shirt on the bed, it would not have wrinkled.
14. Should the children (lie, lay) under the tables during a tornado warning?
15. The crystal was (sat, set) too near the edge of the mantel, and it fell.
16. The children (lay, laid) quietly when it was time for their nap.

17. They had (sat, set) toward the back of the banquet hall but were ushered to the front.

18. (Sit, Set) your sights high and you will accomplish much.

19. We spent most of our vacation (lying, laying) in the sun.

20. Thus far, he has (lain, laid) most of his emphasis on the need for immigration quotas.

Name______________________________ Date_____________ Score___________

ACTIVITY 11-3, VERB FORMS

Fill in the appropriate verb form. The present tense form of the verb or verbs to be used precedes the sentence.

Example: *sit* The student was *sitting* on the grass.

lie 1. The students chose a picnic spot that __________ along the bank of a small creek.

lay 2. They __________ a blanket on the grass and prepared their picnic lunch.

sit/set 3. After everyone __________ on the edge of the blanket, plates of cheese, crackers, and grapes were __________ before them.

lie 4. Next to the blanket were _____________ a frisbee, football, and a deck of cards.

lie/lie 5. After eating, a few of the picnickers chose to __________ on the grass for a short nap, although one jumped up quickly, after discovering that he had __________ in a nest of ants.

sit 6. Others were _____________ on the banks of the creek throwing pebbles into the water.

lie 7. Next to the creek, someone discovered an arrowhead that had ___________ undetected, perhaps for centuries.

lay 8. Two others had ___________ claim to the frisbee and were tossing it back and forth across the creek.

mislay 9. Toward the end of the day, everyone gathered to search for a pair of sunglasses that one student had _________________.

set 10. The sun was ________________ when the students decided to leave.

Write five sentences which make use of the words provided below.

11. lain ____

____

____

12. mislaid ______________________________________

____

____

13. setting ______________________________________

____

____

14. lies ____

____

____

15. laid ____

____

____

12 VERB TENSE

Tense indicates the time sequence of the action or state expressed by a verb. There are six tenses.

The present tense is used for actions that occur in the present, that are habitual or continuous, or that are general in nature.

The student needs a ride home.
Our football team plays every Saturday.
Most people eat a large meal in the evening.
Money is the root of all evil.

The past tense is used for actions that are completed in the past or are habitually in the past.

She lived in Atlanta for six years.
Donna broke her ankle during spring tryouts.
When I spent more time in the library, I invariably raised my grades.

The future tense is used for actions that will occur in the near or distant future.

English class will end in a few minutes.
The sun probably will explode in a supernova within the next 30 billion years.

The **present perfect tense** is used for actions that begin in the past but continue up to the present, actions that are continuous in the past, or actions that occurred at an indefinite time in the past.

> She has lived in Atlanta for six years.
> Most colleges have attempted to recruit the best students.
> He rarely has sought advice when making decisions.

The past perfect tense is used for actions that have been completed prior to another past action.

> The students had studied many hours before they took the test. (They had studied before they took.)

> Before he recovered his speech, he had spent countless hours in therapy. (He had spent before he **recovered**.)

The future perfect tense is used for actions that will be completed before another action or prior to a specified future time.

> Before she has left the pool, she will have swum sixteen kilometers.
> He will have completed the examination by 10:00 on Tuesday.

Progressive Forms

Each verb tense has a progressive form. This form is used to indicate that the action is ongoing or "in progress." Each form makes use of some form of the verb be and the present participle.

Progressive Forms

Present: The student is calling his friend.

Past: She was studying her homework.

Future: The class will be learning cardio-pulmonary resuscitation.

Present Perfect: Have you been visiting her recently?

Past Perfect: I stopped what I had been doing.

Future Perfect: By Thursday, the monk will have been fasting for four days.

12A SHIFTS IN TENSE

Shift from one tense, or time sequence, to another only when there is an actual change in the time sequence of the action. That is, a piece of writing which begins in the present tense should remain so until a change in time necessitates a new tense.

Name______________________________ Date_____________ Score__________

ACTIVITY 12-1, VERB TENSE

Correct the underlined verbs, changing them to the tense or form identified at the end of each sentence. Write the correct form to the left of the numbered item.

Example: *has changed* — Newspaper writing changes over the years. (present perfect)

______________________ 1. Over the years, newspapers provide Americans with a wealth of information. (present perfect)

______________________ 2. News always is a part of a good daily paper. (present perfect)

______________________ 3. Even early papers focused on those events that previously gains the greatest reader interest. (past perfect)

______________________ 4. The papers show little regard for a balanced presentation of news events. (past tense)

______________________ 5. Whatever the ethics of this kind of reporting, this penchant for sensationalism proves economically advantageous. (present perfect)

______________________ 6. Modern newspapers make great use of the feature article. (present progressive tense)

______________________ 7. It is conceivable that papers of the year 2000 include mostly feature articles. (future tense)

______________________ 8. It is true that early journalists write features, but those articles

______________________ do not provide the diversity that modern features do. (past progressive tense; past tense)

______________________ 9. Modern feature articles focus on such topics as biography, travel, finance, society and politics. (present progressive tense)

____________________ 10. Editorial pages of contemporary newspapers also <u>improve</u> over their historical counterparts. (present perfect)

____________________ 11. More than one early paper that claimed to reflect broad popular opinion simply <u>presents</u> a narrow opinion of the publisher. (past progressive)

____________________ 12. The modern reader <u>expects</u> editorial integrity and, if the current trend holds, <u>demands</u> greater integrity in the future. (present progressive; future progressive)

____

Name______________________________ Date_____________ Score___________

ACTIVITY 12-2, VERB TENSE

Provide the correct verb form for each of the following sentences. The present tense of the verb to be used is provided at the end of the sentence.

Example: In the past, reporters *developed* their skills while on the job. (develop)

1. From the early days of the newspaper until the present, every cub reporter ________________ his newspaper career writing obituaries. (begin)

2. A noted journalist once ________________ that he ________________ his now famous style while writing obituaries. (claim, develop)

3. This kind of writing, although dull, still ______________ a new reporter self-discipline. (teach)

4. Before he ends his first year, the new journalist ________________ stories on a countless variety of topics. (write)

5. He will have written detailed investigative reports on topics which he ________________ little about before beginning his journalistic career. (knows)

6. Journalists also have the opportunity for travel; by the end of a year many ________________ as many miles as a professional pilot. (fly)

7. It is not unusual for a good reporter to place odds that by the end of his career he ____________________ over 1,000,000 miles! (travel)

8. It is while traveling to an unknown area to report on one event that a journalist ________________ a lead on a different story. (discover)

9. While flying from New York to Chicago, one ambitious reporter ________________ a feature story on the poor condition of the plane on which he flew! (complete)

10. Although a journalist's pay is meager, many young people over the years ________________ the exciting field of journalism. (enter)

11. All of these people hope that some day their articles ________________ by the major news agencies. (distribute)

12. Every reporter dreams that some story he writes ________________ a Pulitzer prize. (receive)

Name________________________________ Date______________ Score___________

ACTIVITY 12-3, VERB TENSE

Identify the tense and, if appropriate, the form of each of the following verbs. Then write a sentence using the verb provided.

Example: has seen (tense) *present perfect*

Although only three years old, the young child has seen much of the world.

1. will deliver (tense)___________________

____

____

2. swam (tense)___________________

____

____

3. was writing (tense and form)_________________________________

____

____

4. had called (tense)___________________

____

____

5. is studying (tense and form)_________________________________

____

____

6. will have completed (tense)___________________

____

____

7. has lived (tense)________________

____

____

8. began (tense)________________

____

____

9. will have gone (tense)________________

____

____

10. had lain (tense)________________

____

____

11. will be working (tense and form)________________________

____

____

12. Will speak (tense) ________________

____

____

Name______________________________ Date_____________ Score___________

ACTIVITY 12-4, VERB TENSE

Correct any unnecessary shift in verb tense by crossing out incorrect verbs and writing the correct form above.

In writing news articles, most reporters rely on the five W's and the H. That is, a good news story will tell what, who, when, where, why, and how. These questions have provided the general format for a news article and will assist the reporter in getting to the heart of the news. In the past, reporters present this information throughout their news article. Often early reporters will report information in the same order in which they receive it. Now, reporters had presented the five W's and the H in the first paragraph of an article. Thus, they will know that the reader was aware of the basic elements of the news event, even if that reader has read no further than the opening paragraph. The following was a typical lead paragraph which has used the five W format.

> This morning, the FBI searches the city wharf area for Wendy Smith, a four-year-old child who will wander from her parents two days ago. The child apparently leaves her mother's side while her mother had watched an ocean-going vessel as it pulls into the harbor. Divers currently probed the water near the wharf.

13/14 VERB MOOD/ACTIVE AND PASSIVE VOICES

Mood

There are three moods for verbs, each of which reflects a particular intention or attitude of the writer. The indicative mood is used for statements of fact, the imperative mood for commands, and the subjunctive mood for expressing desires, suggestions, or statements contrary to fact. The subjunctive mood is often the least understood.

Indicative

He walked into the room.
I usually read magazines for relaxation.

Imperative

Close the door, please.
Shut up!

Subjunctive

Commonly, the subjunctive makes use of be and were (not am, is, are, or was). It also makes use of present tense verbs without the s.

Uses of the Subjunctive

Commands, Demands

The teacher demanded that Beverly do her work.
She insists that he be here on time.

Wishes, Requests, Preferences

I wish I were a millionaire.
The lawyer requested that the judge overrule the decision.
His wife prefers that he remain silent.

Conditions Contrary to Fact, Conditional Statements

If I were you, I would sell that old car.
Were cancer contagious, we would all be dead.

NOTE: In current usage, primarily in speech and informal writing, the indicative is often substituted for the subjunctive mood.

Active and Passive Voices

The voice of a verb reveals whether the subject does the action indicated by the verb or receives the action indicated by the verb. If the verb is in the active voice, the subject is acting. If the verb is in the passive voice, the subject is acted upon by someone or something else.

Active Voice

(actor) (action)
The woman bought a car.

Passive Voice

(receiver of action) (action)
The car was bought by the woman.

The active voice, which is usually less wordy and more direct, is preferable for most writing. The passive voice is useful if the subject is not identified or is inconsequential.

Name________________________________ Date______________ Score___________

ACTIVITY 13-1, VERB MOOD

The following sentences contain indicative mood verbs. Draw a line through any indicative mood verb which should be subjunctive. Write the correct subjunctive form above the incorrect verb. If the verb moods are correct, write C before the number of the sentence.

Example: It is necessary that every employee ~~is~~ *be* a proficient writer.

1. Many employers insist that new management trainees are effective writers.
2. If the trainee was an employer, he would realize the concern with writing skills.
3. Most business professionals spend over twenty percent of their time writing.
4. Since this situation exists, it is necessary that this writing is clear and understandable.
5. Granted, most businessmen prefer that an intelligent administrative secretary composes the reports and letters.
6. Secretarial personnel, however, do not necessarily have the knowledge required to compose a report.
7. Was this the case, the secretary could easily replace the businessman!
8. Thus, work conditions demand that the mid-level professional has a good grasp of composition techniques and an excellent knowledge of sentence structure.

9. Whether or not the college student wishes to admit it, current needs within the business world necessitate that the student learns as much as he can about correct writing practices.

10. One may prefer that the study of grammar is disregarded; however, practical wisdom suggests that grammar study is taken very seriously.

Name________________________ Date__________ Score________

ACTIVITY 13-2, VERB MOOD

Rewrite the following sentences, changing verbs from the indicative to the subjunctive mood where appropriate.

1. A basic requirement for any business professional is that he is able to write clear business letters.

____

____

2. Was the typical business letter clear, many costly communication problems could be avoided.

____

____

3. Employers expect that business correspondence provides clear, concise information written in a serious manner.

____

____

4. All too often, the business letter reads as if it was a chatty personal letter.

____

____

5. It is no wonder that personnel directors demand that the prospective executive has considerable skill at writing letters.

____

____

6. It is necessary that the business letter indicates its subject in the introductory paragraph.

____

____

7. Was this not the case, the letter could not be easily filed according to its subject.

8. It is also desirable that the letter is clearly typed.

9. Many offices prefer that business letters are no longer than one page.

10. If a person was to produce an ideal business letter, it would be brief, direct, and clear.

Name______________________________ Date_____________ Score___________

ACTIVITY 14-1, ACTIVE AND PASSIVE VOICE

Write sentences which make use of the following verbs. Use the voice specified.

1. celebrate (passive voice)

____

____

2. recognize (active voice)

____

____

3. supply (passive voice)

____

____

4. remove (passive voice)

____

____

5. deliberate (active voice)

____

____

6. expel (passive voice)

____

____

7. awaken (active voice)

____

____

8. publish (active voice)

____

____

9. take (passive voice)

____

____

10. receive (passive voice)

____

____

11. encourage (active voice)

____

____

12. frighten (passive voice)

____

____

Name______________________________ Date____________ Score__________

ACTIVITY 14-2, ACTIVE AND PASSIVE VOICE

Rewrite each sentence, changing the verb from the passive to the active voice. If necessary, provide a new subject for the sentence.

Example: The business report is written by most professionals.

Most professionals write business reports.

1. An effective means of internal communication is needed by every organization.

2. That means of communication is offered by the business report.

3. Proposals for new procedures or descriptions of current processes are effectively presented in business reports.

4. Through a report, information necessary for efficient operations is received by the supervisor.

5. By means of the report, new ideas for more efficient operation are passed on.

6. Many fine ideas presented in conversation are forgotten by the supervisor.

7. The report is effective because through it is provided a permanent record of data and ideas.

8. The report is also valuable in that credit for original ideas is received by the author of the report.

9. Most importantly, however, it is only in a written report that concepts can be fully developed.

10. Thus, chiefly through the report, major issues are debated, and new ideas are disseminated by members of a corporation.

Name______________________________ Date_____________ Score_________

ACTIVITY 14-3, ACTIVE AND PASSIVE VOICE

One form of a verb is provided in each item below. Change the voice of the verb to that specified. Note: The tense of the verb is to remain the same in both voices.

	ACTIVE	PASSIVE
Example:	hit	*was hit*
1.	completed	______
2.	is writing	______
3.	______	has been called
4.	______	will be blessed
5.	had swum	______
6.	was watching	______
7.	______	is bitten
8.	has burned	______
9.	should take	______
10.	______	will have been given
11.	is considering	______
12.	______	will be relocated
13.	has terminated	______
14.	______	will have been counseled
15.	had persuaded	______

15 ADJECTIVES AND ADVERBS

These two parts of speech are modifiers. Adjectives can modify both nouns and pronouns. Adverbs can modify verbs and adjectives, as well as other adverbs. (See Ch. 4.)

Most adjectives and adverbs have three different forms, which are used to express various degrees of intensity. They are the positive, comparative, and superlative degrees.

	Positive	Comparative	Superlative
Adjectives:			
	bad	worse	worst
	good	better	best
	slow	slower	slowest
	happy	happier	happiest
	happy	less happy	least happy
Adverbs:			
	badly	worse	worst
	well	better	best
	slowly	more slowly	most slowly
	slowly	less slowly	least slowly
	happily	more happily	most happily

NOTE: Concepts such as <u>total</u>, <u>unique</u>, <u>empty</u>, and <u>perfect</u> are absolute by nature. These modifiers can have neither comparative nor superlative forms.

The Comparative

This form is used to compare two people or things.

No comparative form makes use of more or less as well as the er suffix. (Incorrect: more slower)

The Superlative

This form is used to differentiate intensity among three or more people or things.

No superlative form will make use of most or least as well as the est suffix. (Incorrect: most happiest)

In most cases (but not all), modifiers ending in ly make use of more and most, rather than er and est. (Incorrect: clearlier)

Adverbs and ly

Often, an adverb is formed by adding **ly** to an adjective. Do not use an adjective when an adverb is needed.

Incorrect
The child whispered quiet.
He handled the explosives very careful.

Revisions

The child whispered quietly.
He handled the explosives very carefully.

NOTE: Some adjectives end in ly: friendly, lonely, fatherly. (See Ch. 4.)

Adjectives

An adjective can follow a linking verb and modify the subject of the sentence.

An adjective can also modify and follow a direct object.

Examples:
The child was curious.
The teachers labeled the child mischievous.

Adverbs

An adverb can modify an action verb, but it need not be placed close to that verb.

Examples:

Quietly, the old man spoke of their long marriage.

She wore her clothes beautifully.

Bad and badly; good and well

Bad and good are adjectives. Both can be used after linking verbs such as feel. (See Ch. 4.)

I feel bad today, but yesterday I felt good.

Badly and well are adverbs and, as such, can modify action verbs, such as did.

I did badly on the first test, but I usually do well on the final.

Well is also an adjective commonly meaning "satisfactory, fortunate, or in good health."

I am well now, and all seems well with the world.

Name______________________________ Date______________ Score_________

ACTIVITY 15-1, ADJECTIVES AND ADVERBS

Provide the appropriate form for the italicized word.

Example:
rapid (comparative adverb) *more rapidly*

1. *sweet* (superlative adjective)_______________
2. *safe* (comparative adverb)_______________
3. *bad* (positive adverb)_______________
4. *perfect* (positive adjective)_______________
5. *angry* (superlative adverb)_______________
6. *poor* (superlative adjective)_______________
7. *bad* (superlative adjective)_______________
8. *sure* (comparative adverb)_______________
9. *unsafe* (superlative adjective)_______________
10. *great* (comparative adverb)_______________
11. *profound* (superlative adjective)_______________
12. *useful* (comparative adjective)_______________
13. *easy* (superlative adverb)_______________
14. *entire* (positive adjective)_______________
15. *little* (comparative adjective)_______________
16. *predictable* (positive adverb)_______________
17. *careful* (superlative adverb)_______________
18. *nice* (comparative adverb)_______________
19. *easy* (superlative adjective)_______________
20. *willing* (comparative adverb)_______________

21. *delightful* (comparative adjective)________________

22. *curious* (superlative adverb)________________

23. *unexpected* (superlative adverb)________________

24. *strong* (comparative adjective)________________

25. *total* (positive adverb)________________

26. *unlawful* (positive adverb)________________

27. *clear* (superlative adjective)________________

28. *preferable* (positive adverb)________________

29. *lonely* (comparative adjective)________________

30. *simple* (comparative adjective)________________

Name______________________________ Date_____________ Score___________

ACTIVITY 15-2, ADJECTIVES AND ADVERBS

Underline the appropriate modifiers in each of the following sentences.

1. How (good, well) athletics and academics mix is a question which many colleges are asking.

2. It is sometimes the case that not the (best, bestest) student but the (more capable, most capable) athlete is awarded scholarship money.

3. There have also been scandals in which (undecided, undecidedly) recruits are "lent" (unbelievable, unbelievably) expensive automobiles.

4. Indeed, recent events suggest that the situation surrounding college athletics has gone from bad to (worse, worst).

5. As a result, proposals that colleges withdraw from intercollegiate competition are being taken more and more (serious, seriously).

6. A major factor, however, in any decision is that athletic programs sometimes bring (considerable, considerably) large sums of money to colleges.

7. Defenders of athletic programs point out (quick, quickly) that the money (sure, surely) is important to both the academic and the athletic elements of the college.

8. In contrast, detractors of athletic programs are (sure, surely) that the money goes (direct, directly) into the athletic budget.

9. Although the financial issue is important, the (importanter, more important) matter relates to the academic program.

10. How (bad, badly) are academics affected by a large athletic program?

11. Then again, is the effect of athletics on the academic program perhaps (good, well)?

12. A major argument against athletic programs is that they recruit (poor, poorly) prepared students.

13. If some athletes are (less prepared, least prepared) than others, the problem can be solved most (effective, effectively) by raising college admission criteria.

14. Then again, if recruiters showed (real, really) interest in the academic progress of the student-athlete, athletic programs would be less (severe, severely) criticized.

15. The problems surrounding the academics and athletics controversy are both (unique, most unique) and significant; thus the consequences of any possible solution should be very (careful, carefully) weighed.

Name____________________________ Date______________ Score__________

ACTIVITY 15-3, ADJECTIVES AND ADVERBS

Rewrite the following sentences, changing the italicized adjectives or adverbs to the comparative or superlative, as indicated. Note: a change in the modifier may require substantial changes in the sentence.

Example: John is *taller* than Jim and *taller* than Ed. (comparative ——> superlative)

Although John, Jim, and Ed are all over six feet, John is the tallest.

1. In many ways, my freshman year in college was a *good* year. (positive ——> superlative)

____

____

2. The hat was *expensive*, as was the ring. (positive ——> comparative)

____

____

3. Helen's beauty was *widely* reported. (positive ——> superlative)

____

____

4. She was known to be *more capable* than the other students. (comparative ——> superlative)

____

____

5. He proceeded *cautiously* this time. (positive ——> comparative)

____

____

6. His situation is bad, but hers is also *bad.*
(positive ⟶ comparative)

____

____

7. Among the names on the list, hers was *prominent.*
(positive ⟶ superlative)

____

____

8. Many spoke harshly of Jim and *harshly* of Sue.
(positive ⟶ superlative)

____

____

9. The pie looked sweet, but the cake tasted *sweet.*
(positive ⟶ comparative)

____

____

10. The one *genuinely* surprised was the youngest child.
(positive ⟶ superlative)

____

____

Name______________________________ Date______________ Score_________

ACTIVITY 15-4, ADJECTIVES AND ADVERBS

Choose the appropriate word form; then write it in the space provided.

Example:
(independent, independently) Some say that athletic programs should operate *independently* of the rest of the college.

(bad, badly)
(good, well)
1. It is not uncommon for a college to do ________________ in academics but ______________ in sports.

(realistic, realistically)
2. Many have suggested that such colleges examine________________ their purpose.

(total, totally)
3. The consensus is that if a choice must be made, the college should be____________ committed to academics.

(cynical, cynically)
(actual, actually)
4. Many skeptics, however, have ________________ noted that a bankrupt college is ___________ no college at all.

(potential, potentially)
5. These people view athletic programs as________________ sources of needed funds.

(obvious, obviously)
(undeniable, undeniably)
6. ________________, some balance must be attained between a college's ________________ demands for funds and its obligation to provide a solid education.

(*necessary, necessarily*) 7. As many colleges have demonstrated, sports programs do not ________________ conflict with academic programs.

(*good, well*) 8. It is possible for students to feel ________________ about an athletic team, even if it is not number one in the nation.

(*bad, badly*) 9. Some consider it ______________ for a college to have a second-rate athletic program.

(*worse, worst*) 10. However, it is far ____________ for a college to have a second-rate academic program.

16 COORDINATION AND SUBORDINATION

Coordination and subordination are methods of constructing sentences which have more than one clause. Coordination exists when all ideas are considered equal in importance and are presented in similar grammatical constructions. Subordination exists when one idea or more are considered less important and are presented in a dependent grammatical construction. (See Clauses, Ch. 5.)

Coordinate Clauses are independent clauses which are linked by a comma and a coordinating conjunction, a semicolon, or sometimes a colon. (Coordinating conjunctions are and, but, or, nor, for, so, yet.)

The mayor met with the commissioners, and the commissioners met with the city administrators.

She ate breakfast; then she left for school.

Bill is more than an employee: he is a friend.

Subordinate Constructions are dependent clauses, phrases, or words which are linked to an independent clause.

We left the party early because we both were tired from the long day's work.

Leaning too far over the railing, the child lost his balance and nearly fell into the reflection pool.

Exhausted, the soldiers rested along the side of the trail.

16A AVOID EXCESSIVE COORDINATION AND SUBORDINATION.

Excessive coordination and subordination are marked by lengthy and confusing sentences. They result from the writer's attempt to put everything down on paper at once--usually in the same sentence.

Excessive coordination is characterized by repeated use of coordinating conjunctions or semicolons to link a number of independent clauses.

> He walked into the house, and he saw that no one else was at home, so he went into the kitchen, and he prepared himself a sandwich; then he went to the den, and he watched television.

Excessive coordination is often corrected by subordinating some ideas and putting others in a different sentence.

> Walking into the house and finding no one home, he went to the kitchen and prepared a sandwich. He then went into the den and watched television.

Excessive subordination is distinguished by an overabundance of often loosely related dependent clauses and phrases within a sentence.

> The restaurants that are most popular are those preparing fresh seafood which is shipped by plane on a daily basis from the coast where boats arrive early in the morning with catches made the night before.

Excessive subordination often is avoided by using more than one sentence or several independent clauses to present a cluster of related ideas.

> The most popular restaurants are those which prepare fresh seafood. The seafood is shipped daily by plane from the coast. It is there that boats arrive early in the morning with the previous night's catches.

Faulty Coordination and Subordination

Faulty coordination and subordination occur when sentence constructions link unrelated ideas, combine ideas in an illogical fashion, or fail to clarify the relationship between ideas.

Faulty coordination exists when unrelated ideas are linked or related ideas are illogically linked.

Faulty Coordination

> The weather was quite pleasant, and the paint that my father bought for the house cost $75.00.
>
> She was exhausted from her lack of sleep, and she seemed to be lively and well rested.

Revisions

> The weather was ideal for painting, so my father began his project by buying $75.00 worth of house paint.
>
> She was exhausted from her lack of sleep; however, she appeared lively and well rested.

Faulty subordination exists when the wrong idea seems to be subordinated or when there is a confusing relationship between the main clause and the subordinate construction.

Faulty Subordination

> Even though he reads a great deal, he has little formal education.
>
> When I ran every morning for sixty minutes, I knew that I would be in shape for the race.

Revisions

> Although he has little formal education, he reads a great deal.
>
> Because I ran every morning for sixty minutes, I knew that I would be in shape for the race.

Name______________________________ Date______________ Score_________

ACTIVITY 16-1, COORDINATION AND SUBORDINATION

The following short sentences can be combined effectively by using a coordinating or subordinating word. Combine the sentences by placing the appropriate word in the blank space and, if necessary, by changing punctuation and correcting capitalization. Choose the appropriate word from those preceding the sentence.

Example:

(and, but) There are large volumes written on Shakespeare's biography., ____*but*____ We actually know very few facts about his life.

(Although, Because) 1. ________________ Shakespeare was christened on April 26, 1564. We generally regard April 23 as his birthdate.

(and, since) 2. He probably did not have a sheltered childhood. ________________ He was one of eight children.

(and, therefore) 3. William's father was a merchant. ________________ He was an active participant in local governmental affairs.

(however, so) 4. The father, John, never signed his name. ________________ Some historians conjecture that he was illiterate.

(where, yet) 5. William probably attended the local school. ________________ He studied many of the classical dramatists.

(Even though, If) 6. ________________ He saw plays as a youngster. They were presented by the traveling acting companies that passed through his town.

(Because, When) 7. ________________ Shakespeare was in his twenties. He went to London to become a playwright.

(for, but) 8. He had to go to London to sell his plays.________________He knew that his small town would not provide financial support for a playwright.

(Since, While) 9. ________________he was in London. His wife and children apparently remained in their hometown, Stratford.

(therefore, however) 10. William became a very successful London playwright.________________he always considered Stratford his home.

Name______________________________ Date______________ Score_________

ACTIVITY 16-2, COORDINATION AND SUBORDINATION

The following sentences can be combined effectively by making use of coordinating and subordinating constructions. Combine each group of sentences into one or two longer sentences.

Example: William Shakespeare is famous. He is an English playwright. He lived in the sixteenth century.

William Shakespeare is a famous English playwright who lived in the sixteenth century.

1. We know little of Shakespeare's personal life. We know he was married. He married Anne Hathaway.

____

____

2. They were married on November 27, 1582. William was eighteen. Anne was twenty-six.

____

____

3. The Shakespeares had three children. Susanna was the oldest daughter. Hamnet and Judith were twins.

____

____

4. Hamnet died as a child. Susanna and Judith lived full lives. Susanna and Judith both married.

____

____

5. Shakespeare was probably in London in the early 1590's. He remained there for approximately twenty years. He wrote his plays and poetry while in London.

____

____

6. Shakespeare wrote long narrative poems. He wrote short lyric poems. He is best known for his plays.

---

7. In the early 1590's the playhouses were closed. At that time the young Shakespeare could not make money writing plays. He wrote poetry.

---

8. Shakespeare was associated with a leading acting company. He was a member of the Lord Chamberlain's Company. This company performed many of his plays.

---

9. Shakespeare wrote history plays and comedies. His great plays are his tragedies. King Lear and Hamlet are tragedies.

---

10. Shakespeare was not well-educated. He was not born into the aristocracy. His plays reveal his true creative genius.

Name__________________________ Date____________ Score________

ACTIVITY 16-3, COORDINATION AND SUBORDINATION

Rewrite the following sentences, correcting any problems with excessive or faulty coordination or subordination. Construct shorter or longer sentences, as necessary.

Example: William Shakespeare was a child and he probably attended the Stratford grammar school and he probably did not attend Oxford University.

As a child, William Shakespeare probably attended the Stratford grammar school. He probably did not attend Oxford University.

1. William Shakespeare went to school, and he read plays, but he didn't read Shakespeare's Plays, but he read the classical writers.

2. He read mostly the classical Latin writers who were well known, because he did not read many Greek writers because they were not well known.

3. School days for Shakespeare, which were very long, began at 6 or 7 in the morning with two breaks, which were for breakfast and lunch, and ended at 5 or 6 in the afternoon, and lasted six days a week and continued for most of the year.

4. Shakespeare made use of the five-act structure in his own plays, but this structure was used by the Roman dramatists, whom he read in grammar school.

____

____

____

____

5. Shakespeare studied grammar, and he studied logic, and he studied rhetoric, which included literature, and he studied some Greek, although he probably did not study much Greek.

____

____

____

____

Name______________________________ Date_____________ Score__________

ACTIVITY 16-4, COORDINATION AND SUBORDINATION

Complete the following sentences by adding a suitable main clause.

Example: Because there was little opportunity to write plays in Stratford, *Shakespeare moved to London.*
____

1. Although there are many biographies written on William Shakespeare, ____
____

2. When they were married William Shakespeare was 18; however, ____
____

3. Because the theatres were closed in the 1590's,
____
____

4. Before Shakespeare moved to London, __________________________
____

5. After Shakespeare studied plays with a five-act structure, ____
____

6. Although Hamnet died as a child, ____________________________
____

7. While Shakespeare lived in London, ___________________________
____

8. Even though Shakespeare was not extremely well-educated, ______________________________

____

9. Whenever students read Shakespeare, ______________________________

____

____

10. If Shakespeare were alive today ______________________________

____

____

17 ILLOGICAL SENTENCES

Some sentences are confusing or unclear because elements within the sentence seem unreasonable or because there seems to be no logical relationship among the various elements of the sentence. Sentences must contain complete and reasonably presented assertions. It is not the reader's job to repair faulty thinking found in a sentence.

Certain errors often result in illogical sentences and are to be avoided.

17A AVOID FAULTY COMPARISONS.

Incomplete comparisons

> A good speech has more examples. (More examples than what?)

Revision

> A good speech has more examples than does the speech he delivered.

Inexact comparisons

> Alaska is larger than any state in the United States. (Alaska is in the U.S. and cannot be larger than itself.)

Revision

Alaska is larger than any <u>other</u> state in the United States.

Illogical comparison

Her knowledge of the law is equal to a judge. (To compare her knowledge and the judge himself makes no sense.)

Revision

Her knowledge of law is equal to a judge's.

or

Her knowledge of law is equal to that of a judge.

Ambiguous comparison

She scolded the child more than his father. (It is unclear whether she scolded the child and his father or whether she scolded the child more than the child's father did.)

Revision

She scolded the child more than his father scolded him.

Interrupted comparisons

I like his car as well, if not better, than my own. (The comparison, which should be "as well as," is incomplete. The resulting "as well . . . than my own" makes no sense.)

He owns one of the largest, if not the largest, house in town. (He may own "one of the largest houses" or "the largest house." He cannot own "one of the largest house.")

Revisions

I like his car as well as my own, if not better than mine.

He owns one of the largest houses in town, if not the largest.

17B AVOID FAULTY APPOSITION.

Be certain that the appositive actually renames or reidentifies the noun to which it refers.

Faulty appositive

She was married in a very special wedding gown, her mother.

William had one overriding desire: a scientist.

Revision

She was married in a very special wedding gown, her mother's.

William had one overriding desire: to be a scientist.

17C AVOID FAULTY PREDICATION AND ILLOGICAL PREDICATE NOUNS.

Illogical

The meaning of the paper was difficult to read because of the poor handwriting. (The paper, not the meaning, was difficult to read.)

I speak English, and he Chinese. (The verb <u>speak</u> is not suitable for the third person singular pronoun <u>he</u>.)

Revisions

Because poor handwriting made the paper difficult to read, I could not grasp its meaning.

I speak English, and he speaks Chinese.

Illogical

His hobby was a stamp collector. (Stamp collecting is a hobby!)

The reason I quit was because I was exhausted. (<u>Because</u> is redundant when used with <u>reason</u>.)

Revisions

His hobby was stamp collecting.

The reason I quit was <u>that</u> I was exhausted.
or
I quit because I was exhausted.

Illogical

A supernova is when a star explodes. (A supernova <u>is</u> something that <u>occurs</u> at a particular time.)

Geology is where you study the surface and structure of the earth. (Geology is not a place; thus <u>where</u> is inappropriate.)

Revisions

A supernova is the explosion of a star.
or
A supernova occurs when a star explodes.

Geology is the study of the surface and structure of the earth.

17D AVOID INCORRECT PREPOSITIONS.

Illogical

The parents were conscious and worried about the child's eating habits.

Revisions

The parents were conscious <u>of</u> and worried <u>about</u> the child's eating habits.

17E AVOID GARBLED SENTENCES.

When one section of a sentence is corrected or in some way changed, other elements of a sentence may be affected. Be certain to proofread sentences to avoid confusing omissions, transposed elements, or illogical subject-verb combinations.

Name________________________ Date____________ Score________

ACTIVITY 17-1, ILLOGICAL SENTENCES

Identify each of the following sentences as logical in construction (L) or faulty in construction (F). Check for problems with comparisons, appositives, predication, and prepositions.

Example:

__F__ A job that requires skill and dedication is a border patrol officer.

_____ 1. Today, a border patrol officer is a more well-known profession.

_____ 2. There is a demand for border patrol officers because the United States has more unpatrolled border than any nation on earth.

_____ 3. The job of the border patrol is made up of men and women working for the federal government.

_____ 4. The job of the border patrol officer is as important as that of any other federal officer, and perhaps more important than the jobs of many.

_____ 5. Searching for illegal immigrants, the border patrol officer checks cars, luggage, and even purses.

_____ 6. The reason the job is important is because many of the illegal drugs sold in the United States come from outside the country's borders.

_____ 7. Just as important than illegal drugs are unwanted infestations that can enter the country with imported plants and animals.

_____ 8. In fact, the arrival of an infestation such as the fruit fly is a small insect that can destroy millions of dollars worth of crops.

_____ 9. Thus, much of the contraband looked and confiscated by the border patrol officers is in the form of exotic plants.

_____ 10. The border patrol officer's job can be more exciting than anyone else and can also be very rewarding.

Write sentences which make use of the constructions indicated below.

11. (more . . . than any other . . . .)

12. (as tall as . . . if not taller than . . . .)

13. (conscious of . . . and worried about . . . .)

14. (most expensive . . . .)

15. (one of the most . . . if not the most . . . .)

Name________________________ Date__________ Score________

ACTIVITY 17-2, ILLOGICAL SENTENCES

Rewrite each sentence, correcting faulty comparisons.

Example: The United States has the largest number of immigrants than any other country.

The United States has a larger number of immigrants than any other country.

1. The rate at which people are immigrating into the U. S. far exceeds emigrants.

____

____

2. The larger number of immigrants comes from the Hispanic countries of South America.

____

____

3. Texas has one of the largest, if not the largest, number of immigrants each year.

____

____

4. Many employers hire immigrants more quickly.

____

____

5. They believe that the immigrant's skills are as good, or better than a domestic worker.

____

____

6. Others feel that the influx of immigrants will cause the U. S. to have a higher unemployment rate than any industrialized nation.

7. These people believe that large numbers of immigrants will make the average wage as small, if not smaller than the wage in developing countries.

8. Immigration officials in Canada are less concerned with Central American immigrants than North Americans.

9. Canada's population is much smaller than America.

10. Canada's unused land is equal, if not greater than, the United States.

Name______________________________ Date____________ Score________

ACTIVITY 17-3, ILLOGICAL SENTENCES

Rewrite each sentence, correcting faulty appositions, faulty comparisons, faulty predication, faulty prepositions, and any other problem that results in an illogical sentence construction.

Example: The many causes of the increase of immigrants are difficult to stop.

It is difficult to determine the many causes of the increase in immigration.

1. America is a diverse and vibrant nation because of one group's contribution, the immigrant.

____

____

2. Most who now live in the U.S. are the grandchildren or great-grandchildren of immigration.

____

____

3. The reason why many Americans are now concerned is because of the new wave of recent immigrants.

____

____

4. The backgrounds of some of the recent immigrants from Cuba were criminals.

____

____

5. In some few instances, certain South Americans deal and are guilty of drugs.

____

____

6. Unfortunately the feeling of many Americans stereotyped all immigrants because of a few.

7. In reality, most immigrants contribute as much, if not more, tax dollars than other Americans.

8. Many immigrants enter quite respectable professions like doctors, lawyers, businessmen, and teachers.

9. The strength of America is when new cultures bring in new ideas and new craftsmen.

10. In short, the increase of immigrants brings into America much more as they take from it.

18 MODIFIERS

Modifiers are effective only if they clearly refer to the words which they modify. Faulty use of modifiers can result in confusing, even incoherent, sentences.

18A CORRECT DANGLING MODIFIERS.

Some modifiers at first appear to modify a particular word, yet a second reading reveals that they actually modify nothing directly stated within the sentence. They are dangling, often at the beginning or end of the sentence, with no grammatical link to the rest of the sentence.

Dangling modifiers

> Losing sixteen pounds, her clothes began to look baggy. (Clothes do not lose sixteen pounds.)
>
> Although annoyed by the waiter, the meal was delicious. (People, not meals, become annoyed.)

Revisions

> Losing sixteen pounds, she found that her clothes began to look baggy.
>
> Although we were annoyed by the waiter, we found the meal to be delicious.

18B CORRECT MISPLACED MODIFIERS.

Avoid confusion by placing prepositional phrases, participial phrases, and adjective clauses as close as possible to the words being modified.

Avoid using a long modifier to separate major sentence elements such as the subject from its verb, or verb from its complement, or verb parts. Long interrupting phrases or clauses can cause the sentence to be confusing.

Misplaced modifiers

The police chief is a man of few words in our town. (According to this sentence, while he is in town, the chief does not speak much.)

The young hoodlums often mug the unsuspecting elderly roaming the city's streets. (It is not characteristic of the elderly to roam city streets.

One woman blamed rising unemployment and increasing taxes on the governor, who remained unidentified. (Who is it that is unidentified?)

The child was, although lost from his parents for two days in the middle of January, unharmed.

Revisions

The police chief in our town is a man of few words.

The young hoodlums roaming the city's streets often mug the unsuspecting elderly.

One woman, who remained unidentified, blamed rising unemployment and increasing taxes on the governor.

Although lost from his parents for two days in the middle of January, the child was unharmed.

NOTE: An adverbial modifier is misplaced if it appears between the two parts of an infinitive. An infinitive is composed of to plus the verb (i.e., to run, to sleep, to go); however, an infinitive functions grammatically as one word. Avoid split infinitives: that is, infinitives whose parts are divided by adverbs. (Incorrect: to quickly run, to quietly sleep, to slowly go.)

18C CORRECT AMBIGUOUS MODIFIERS.

An ambiguous modifier is in such a position that it obscures the meaning of the sentence. Words such as almost, hardly, any, just, only, and nearly present particular problems.

Ambiguous

> We just visited England.
>
> He only talks about golf.

Revisions

> We just visited England; we didn't live there.

or

> We visited just England, not France.
>
> He doesn't play golf; he only talks about it.

or

> Because no other sport interests him, he talks only about golf.

A squinting modifier appears to modify either a word that precedes it or one that follows. Correct the problem by moving the modifier closer to the word being modified.

Squinting

> The automobile that he bought recently has given him problems. (Recently bought, or recently giving problems?)
>
> She promised before taking office to divest herself of out-of-state investments. (Was the promise made before taking office, or is the divestiture to take place before she takes office?)

Revisions

> The recently purchased automobile has given him problems.

or

The automobile that he bought has given him problems recently.

Before taking office, she promised to divest herself of out-of-state investments.

or

She promised to divest herself before taking office of out-of-state investments.

Name________________________ Date____________ Score________

ACTIVITY 18-1, MODIFIERS

Underline any dangling, misplaced, or ambiguous modifiers in the following sentences. If the sentence contains no problems with modifiers, write C before the number of the sentence.

1. Many entering students are not certain of their career fields, who attend college.
2. However, deciding on a career is not as important as one might think during the first years of college.
3. Many careers selected by students after much thought are abandoned for a quite different career.
4. In fact, although confident of their first choices, most early career decisions nevertheless are changed before graduation.
5. A career choice will be correct which is suited to a person's aptitude and interest.
6. A guidance counselor, since that person is especially qualified to discuss matters related to career choices and can provide the student with tests which indicate career preferences, can be of valuable assistance to the student.
7. The findings of the career preference test which the counselor provides for some students may offer important information regarding career potential.
8. Such tests, which are typically inexpensive, easily can be completed in an hour or two.
9. Once a student's aptitude and interests are better known, the counselor can begin to carefully discuss careers which match the student's strengths and interests.
10. Knowing the best area, change is often sensible.
11. To unhappily continue in an unfulfilling profession is a situation which all should avoid.
12. Looking to the future, the computer field may seem very attractive to many.

13. However, the monetary gains for a person mean very little, who does not enjoy her work.

14. The salary is satisfactory almost in any field if a person truly enjoys his work.

15. Remember, it is not the prestige of a career but the personal satisfaction which should be a deciding factor in any career choice.

Name______________________________ Date______________ Score_________

ACTIVITY 18-2, MODIFIERS

Revise each sentence, correcting any problems with faulty modifiers.

Example: A career choice will usually be sensible which matches a person's skills to the market's demand.

A career choice which matches a person's skills to the market's demands will usually be sensible.

1. Any student should first take an inventory of his skills, who wishes to determine the career for which he is most suited.

____

____

2. Realizing that her aptitude is in mathematics, such career areas as engineering, industrial research, or computer science might be given consideration.

____

____

3. If, on the other hand, a student only is interested in English, then he might consider careers which emphasize communication skills.

____

____

4. The businessman who communicates frequently relies on those skills that are learned in English courses.

____

____

5. Students might also consider home decorating, advertising, or architecture with artistic talent.

____

____

6. Science presents important career opportunities, with a strong interest in natural phenomena.

___

___

7. Many students combine several talents to successfully create unique career opportunities.

___

___

8. One recent graduate became an information officer for a company having a background in theatre and economics.

___

___

9. With talents in both art and biology, a company manufacturing anatomical models was very interested.

___

___

10. Employment will, if the person has skills which are needed by a corporation, always be available.

___

___

Name______________________________ Date_____________ Score_________

ACTIVITY 18-3, MODIFIERS

Combine the following clauses, phrases, and words so that each modifier is used in a clear and effective way.

Example: the young person
about the world of business
fresh from college
has much to learn

The young person fresh from college has much to learn about the world of business.

1. that is being offered
employers search
whose credentials match the job
for a candidate

____

____

2. no employer
who does not communicate well
will hire a person
whatever his credentials
in the job interview

____

____

3. relying on past experience
a candidate
who cannot write well
an intelligent personnel director will avoid

____

____

4. also, most employers realize
in a sales position
who constantly meets people
that an employee
must be articulate

5. a bank trainee
only
who relies
on accounting skills
may drive away customers

6. seeking to be efficient
buried in accounting ledgers
may be insensitive to the customer
a new trainee
asking for an educational loan

7. a good employee realizes
of their responsibility
involves their technical skills
that only one part

8. those new employees
have a good rapport with customers
whatever their expertise
who advance most quickly
and with fellow employees

9. an astute communicator
often
also realizes that
to be a good listener
it is best

10. one must understand
all in all
demands personal skills
that the business world
and professional expertise

---

19 SENTENCE CONSISTENCY

Attention to several key elements can lend overall consistency to a sentence. Those elements include verb and pronoun forms, the level of formality, and the point of view.

19A AVOID UNNECESSARY SHIFTS IN VERB FORMS.

Improper combining of can and the conditionals (might, could, should, and would)

> Our performance might improve if we can spend more time preparing.

Revision

> Our performance might improve if we could spend more time preparing.

Unnecessary shifts in voice

From active to passive

> She chooses a design; then the mural is painted.

Revision

> She chooses a design and then paints the mural.

Unnecessary shifts in mood

From Indicative to Imperative

> First, a student should determine a topic; once a topic is determined, begin your research.

Revision

> First, a student should determine a topic; once he has determined the topic, he should begin the research.

From Subjunctive to Indicative

> Membership requires that you attend meetings and that you are active in all fund-raising projects.

Revision

> Membership requires that you attend meetings and that you be active in all fund-raising projects.

From Indicative to Interrogative

> I asked him for directions, and where can I get a good meal?

Revision

> I asked him for directions and asked where I could get a good meal.

19B AVOID INAPPROPRIATE SHIFTS IN THE LEVEL OF FORMALITY.

Slang terms, even when surrounded by quotation marks, are usually unsuitable for formal writing.

Shift

> Although he lived in a poor neighborhood, he drove a "real bad" car.

Revision

> Although he lived in a poor neighborhood, he drove a high performance car.

19C AVOID UNNECESSARY SHIFTS IN THE POINT OF VIEW.

A piece of writing which begins in the third person (she, it, he, they) should remain consistent throughout. Generally, the third person and, in some instances, the first are suitable for collegiate and professional writing.

Unnecessary shift in point of view

> When a student enrolls in a chemistry class, you should be prepared for long hours of study.

Revision

> When a student enrolls in a chemistry class, he should be prepared for long hours of study.

19D AVOID SHIFTS IN NUMBER.

Shifts

> After an athlete finishes a workout, they should cool down slowly.

Revision

> After an athlete finishes a workout, she should cool down slowly.

Name______________________________ Date_____________ Score__________

ACTIVITY 19-1, SENTENCE CONSISTENCY

Underline those words or phrases which contain inappropriate shifts. If the sentence is correct, place a C next to the number of the sentence.

Example: It is necessary that a student understand a library's resources and utilizes them.

1. A library is not simply a storage place for books; a number of services are offered by the library.
2. If a person is to make full use of a library, it is necessary that the person first obtain a library card then uses it.
3. Library holdings include recent international journals and newspapers while many research tools are also included.
4. Browse through the audio-visual section, and one soon realizes that a library houses many films.
5. One might even spend hours listening to the library's recordings, if one can afford the time.
6. The reference section is an important part of the library, for in it are contained data related to practically every field.
7. Whatever a person's professional interest, he can find relevant information in the reference section.
8. By referring to volumes in the reference section, a stock broker can discover why is one stock better than the other.
9. A person who might wonder whether he can sell a new invention can find patent information through reference books.
10. With its many features, a library clearly is an important resource.

Complete the following sentences. Be conscious of sentence consistency from one clause to the next.

11. If students are going to do advanced research in college,

____

____

12. I often study in the library because____________________

____

____

13. You may choose to listen to recordings while at the library, or________________________________

____

____

14. It is necessary that one research a project completely and_____________________________________

____

____

____

15. Read all research material very carefully, and

____

____

Name______________________________ Date______________ Score_________

ACTIVITY 19-2, SENTENCE CONSISTENCY

Rewrite the following sentences, correcting consistency problems which arise from shifts in verb forms, levels of formality, and point of view.

Example: A library can be an important information source for a researcher, if the researcher knows how to use them.

A library can be an important information source for a researcher if he knows how to use it.

1. If one needs information on practically any subject, go first to the library.

____

____

2. The search for information begins with the card catalogue since they contain listings of every book in the library.

____

____

3. Another important publication is the serial catalogue; information related to journals and periodicals is contained in it.

____

____

____

4. The various card catalogues make library material quite accessible even though the volume of information contained within the library is "totally awesome!"

____

____

____

5. If one has a particularly difficult research problem, they should seek the assistance of the reference librarian.

___

___

6. For example, if one who has need of population information and where can she find it, she should speak with the reference librarian.

___

___

7. Although it might take a person two hours to find relevant material, it can take a reference librarian only minutes.

___

___

8. A reference librarian, however, is familiar with the library's materials, and they can move quickly to the book which is most suited to solve the problem.

___

___

___

9. With a librarian's help, a person can solve any problem that they encounter.

___

___

10. Library research demands only that the person be able to spend time among books and that she is willing to read conscientiously about a subject.

___

___

___

Name________________________________ Date______________ Score_________

ACTIVITY 19-3, SENTENCE CONSISTENCY

The following paragraph contains a number of inappropriate shifts which affect consistency. Correct each problem by crossing out unsuitable words or phrases and writing the correct words above the line.

The Sumerians perfected the art of writing approximately 5,000 years ago, and written records were kept in their temples. From these origins, people with brains have traced the development of the library. There are some noteworthy libraries throughout history; you should consider, for example, the library at Alexandria. This library existed about 300 B.C. in Alexandria, Egypt, and more than 900,000 volumes, mostly in Greek, were held by it.

John Harvard founded the first American library, and I learned that the founding of Harvard University was in 1638. In 1731, Benjamin Franklin founded the Library Company of Philadelphia where you could read books if you were a member. In the nineteenth century, local governments asked their constituents would they approve of a tax-supported public library. Take note of 1854, for it was then that Boston opened its public library. Since the library's early establishment in the United States, they have flourished. Currently, there are over 30,000 libraries located in the United States and Canada, of which about 8,000 are found to be public libraries. If citizens can realize the importance of libraries to their community, then they would continue to support the public library.

20 EMPHASIS AND VARIETY

A good piece of writing is lively and engaging. There is nothing duller than the tedious presentation of ideas in unvaried sentence constructions. Effective sentences emphasize main ideas while subordinating less important points. Interesting writing incorporates sentences which use a variety of patterns.

EMPHASIS

20A ACHIEVE EMPHASIS THROUGH ECONOMY OF WORDS.

Include only related ideas in the sentence. Avoid circumlocution and redundancy.

Wordy sentences

> The book about which he spoke is relatively new and deals with the subject of mathematics.
>
> If you will refer back to page number 321, you will find on that page that the major character is over six feet tall.

Revision

> He spoke to us about a new mathematics book.
>
> If you will refer to page 321, you will find that the major character is over six feet tall.

20B ACHIEVE EMPHASIS THROUGH PROPER SUBORDINATION.

Subordination involves presenting in dependent clauses ideas other than the main idea of the sentence (See Ch. 16). By using subordination, a writer can provide proper emphasis for the main idea.

> The convicted murderer was denied a retrial, and he was executed on Friday.

Revised for proper emphasis

> The convicted murderer was executed on Friday after being denied a retrial.

20C ACHIEVE EMPHASIS THROUGH EFFECTIVE REPETITION.

Repetition, if sparingly used, can be a good method of providing emphasis. If overly used, however, repetition makes for verbose writing.

> She looked forward to a new year and beginning.

> Art was both a hobby and a vital emotional therapy.

Revised for emphasis

> She looked forward to a new year and a new beginning.

> Art was not only an interest; art was a vital emotional therapy.

20D ACHIEVE EMPHASIS THROUGH USE OF PARALLELISM.

Similar ideas are best presented in similar, or parallel, grammatical constructions. Parallelism indicates the equality of two or more ideas while emphasizing their relationship. Nonparallel constructions often are confusing.

Nonparallel constructions

> Visiting relatives, to sightsee, and when we relaxed took up most of our vacation time.

> The young girls enjoy their drives around town and waving to friends.

He is a person with honesty and who is fair.

Revisions

Visiting relatives, sightseeing, and relaxing took up most of our vacation time.

The young girls enjoy driving around town and waving to friends.

He is a person who is honest and fair.

20E ACHIEVE EMPHASIS THROUGH USE OF CONTRAST.

She was tall and strikingly attractive.

It takes desire and perseverance to earn a college degree.

Revised for emphasis

She was <u>not only</u> tall <u>but also</u> strikingly beautiful.

Desire is insufficient to earn a college degree <u>unless</u> it is wedded to perseverance.

Variety

20F ACHIEVE VARIETY WITH SENTENCE BEGINNINGS.

Introductory absolute constructions

<u>Our textbook</u> completed, we began advanced study of algebra.

Introductory adjectives or adverbs

<u>Homeless and hungry</u>, the runaway child is easily exploited by unethical adults.

<u>Slowly yet flawlessly</u>, Grandmother stitched together the child's dress.

Introductory appositive

<u>A Triple Crown</u> winner, Secretariat may be the greatest racehorse that ever lived.

Introductory infinitive

To maintain fitness, one should exercise three times a week for thirty minutes.

Introductory dependent clause

After she delivered her speech, the crowd stood to applaud. (Adverb clause)

Why people vandalize public buildings is beyond me. (Noun clause)

Introductory prepositional phrase

In the midst of the dilemma, someone came up with a perfect solution.

Introductory participle

Using the Heimlich hold, the waiter dislodged the food.

20G ACHIEVE VARIETY BY USING DIFFERENT SENTENCE TYPES.

Simple sentences with compound parts

Paper airplanes and old cars were his favorite hobbies. (Compound subjects)

She designed a city and built it in Saudi Arabia. (Compound predicates)

The paramedics rescued both the child and his mother. (Compound direct object)

Compound Sentence

A compound sentence is composed of two independent clauses.

The plane crash-landed, yet no one was hurt.

The children ran into the back yard to play, and the parents chatted over a glass of iced tea.

Complex Sentence

A complex sentence is composed of an independent clause and one or more dependent clauses (i.e., adverb, adjective, or noun clause).

> After she spoke to the store's manager, she wrote the company.
>
> The starting pitcher, who had walked three batters by the end of the second inning, was relieved.
>
> The outstanding student knows that the library is the real student center.

Compound-Complex Sentence

A compound-complex sentence contains two independent clauses and one or more dependent clauses.

> Before he left, he called for his dog, but the animal had run away.
>
> The union threatened to strike, but the company was unconcerned since it had large supplies of its product in storage.

20H ACHIEVE VARIETY USING DIFFERENT SENTENCE STRUCTURES.

The cumulative sentence structure follows the natural order of subject, verb, and modifiers.

> The boxer fell to the canvas, unconscious for the count of ten.

The periodic sentence structure inverts the natural order, not presenting the main clause until the end of the sentence.

> Donning his graduation robes with intense satisfaction and glancing once more toward his parents, who encouraged him throughout college, the young man sauntered out to join his classmates.

The balanced sentence structure counterpoises similar ideas in similar grammatical constructions.

> With proper training, even a sixty year old finds a marathon achievable; without proper training, even a twenty year old finds a mile run exhausting.

20I ACHIEVE VARIETY BY ALTERING SENTENCE LENGTH.

Note how effective a short sentence can become when positioned next to a longer sentence.

> The child shuffled his feet, muttered something, and looked toward the window as if searching for the answer somewhere in the trees outside. He had not studied.

Name______________________________ Date_____________ Score_________

ACTIVITY 20-1, EMPHASIS AND VARIETY

Rewrite the following sentences so that major ideas receive proper emphasis. Rely upon the suggestion in parentheses.

Example: English is the language of business today, and it may not be in the future. (use subordination)

Although English is the language of business today, it may not be in the future.

1. Not many of us, in fact, only a very few, understand that the study and learning of a foreign language other than our own may be essential for the professional businessman of the 1990's. (avoid wordiness)

____

____

____

2. Many immigrants of the past spoke English, and current immigrants speak Spanish or in some instances, Chinese. (use contrast)

____

____

3. It is not currently the case, and in forty years the largest minority population in the U.S. will be Hispanic. (use subordination)

____

____

4. The immigrant will gain economic power, and speaking the immigrant's language will become more important to the businessman. (use subordination)

____

____

5. Most business executives know that the best language for commerce is of the buyer. (use repetition)

____

____

6. Whether the buyer is Chinese, or if he speaks English, or is an Hispanic, the successful company will not allow language to become an obstacle to communication. (use parallelism)

____

____

____

7. A knowledge of language is important, and a knowledge of customs is important. (use contrast)

____

____

8. In Saudi Arabia, a two-cocktail business lunch is not only inappropriate but also irreligious and illegal. (use repetition)

____

____

9. For some people from different cultures in the world, it is very important that a personal friendship be established between the buyer and businessman before any transaction of business begins. (avoid wordiness)

____

____

10. The salesman's religion, what he believes politically, and whether he is married can also influence buyers from other cultures. (use parallelism)

____

____

Name________________________ Date__________ Score_________

ACTIVITY 20-2, EMPHASIS AND VARIETY

Combine each pair of sentences below, changing the first sentence into the kind of phrase or clause indicated. Note: Be certain that the main clause has an identifiable subject.

Example: He ate dinner. Then he went for a walk. (prepositional phrase)

After dinner he went for a walk.

____

1. The new teacher entered the room. The children suddenly fell silent. (absolute phrase)

____

____

2. The lady was looking for Main Street. She drove from one side of town to the other. (participial phrase)

____

____

3. Frank Lloyd Wright was a great American architect. Frank Lloyd Wright is considered an innovator in design. (appositive)

____

____

4. He wanted to save his friend. He dived into the icy lake. (infinitive phrase)

____

____

5. He saw the movie. He understood why it was critically acclaimed. (dependent clause)

____

____

6. The lion was swift and ferocious. It attacked the gazelle. (introductory adverbs)

---

7. The summer house was battered by the storm. It was in great need of repair. (participial phrase)

---

8. The plane went above the clouds. It was suddenly bathed in bright rays of run. (prepositional phrase)

---

9. He delivered his speech. He then sat down for the meal. (absolute phrase)

---

10. The shoes were muddy and wet. They were in no condition to be worn to a party. (introductory adjectives)

---

11. She wanted to satisfy her children. She bought them each an ice cream. (infinitive phrase)

---

12. The sorcerer did not have his wand. He could not perform his magic. (prepositional phrase)

---

13. She was very sick. She enjoyed visits from her friends. (dependent clause)

---

14. He did not notice that the fire was turned on. He touched the hot kettle. (participial phrase)

---

15. Gregor Mendel was the father of modern genetics. He was an Austrian priest with an interest in plants. (appositive)

Name________________________ Date____________ Score__________

ACTIVITY 20-3, EMPHASIS AND VARIETY

Combine the following groups of sentences, making use of the sentence construction indicated.

Example: Languages are influenced by other languages. They change constantly. (compound predicate)

Languages are influenced by other languages and therefore change constantly.

1. Germanic languages influenced the development of English. Romance languages influenced the development of English. (compound subject)

____

____

2. The Angles, Saxons, and Jutes were three Germanic tribes. They invaded England in the fifth century. (complex sentence using an adjective clause)

____

____

3. Britain was occupied by the Romans before the invasion of the Germanic tribes. The Roman occupation did not have a significant influence on the language. (compound sentence)

____

____

4. The Germanic invaders brought a new political order to England. They also brought a new language. (compound direct object)

____

____

5. The Germanic roots of our language are apparent in some verb forms. They are perhaps chiefly apparent in our vocabulary. (complex sentence using an adverb clause)

____

____

6. Words such as *wife, child,* and *house* derive from the language of the Angles and Saxons. Even the name of our language, English, refers to the Angles, or Anglish people. (compound sentence)

____

____

7. The next language to influence English was Latin. Its influence was initially limited to the language of the gentry. Latin was the language of the educated class. (compound-complex sentence)

____

____

8. Greek had less of an influence than Latin. It also influenced the development of the English language. (complex sentence using an adverb clause)

____

____

9. English assimilated certain suffixes from Latin. It also gained a number of new words. (compound predicate)

____

____

10. French was the language of the court after the Norman invasion. It also influenced the development of our language. (complex sentence using an adjective clause)

____

____

Name______________________________ Date____________ Score__________

ACTIVITY 20-4, EMPHASIS AND VARIETY

Combine the following sentence groups, using the kind of sentence structure indicated.

Example: Quiet people are admired for being intelligent. As for people who talk, they are often criticized for being foolish. (balanced)

Quiet people are admired for being intelligent; talkative people are often criticized for being foolish.

1. The mountain climber gripped the rope. He hoped that someone would hear his shout. He hoped that someone would rescue him. (cumulative)

____

____

2. His face was unshaven. His eyes were swollen from lack of sleep. He was in no condition to attend the press conference. (periodic)

____

____

3. One should read because reading provides knowledge. What a person knows gives him a kind of freedom. (balanced)

____

____

4. The players retired to the locker room. They were bruised and exhausted. They had been beaten by two touchdowns. (cumulative)

____

____

5. The plant was watered daily. The plant was protected from the cold March nights. It soon flourished in the spring warmth. (periodic)

____

____

6. The student wasted his time. He sat in the student center. He chatted to whoever passed by. (cumulative)

____

____

7. Babysitters have little trouble with some children. Other children cause a great deal of trouble. (balanced)

____

____

8. The child feared the dark. She was unwilling to admit her fear to her friends. She walked bravely down the dark alley. (periodic)

____

____

9. The President demanded that the foreign ambassador provide an explanation. He knew that the ambassador could not reveal the true reason for his country's actions. (cumulative)

____

____

____

10. Some students will learn as much as they can from a class. In some classes, there are students who learn as little as possible. (balanced)

____

____

21/22 COMMA AND SUPERFLUOUS COMMAS

The comma is the most frequently used mark of internal punctuation.

21A USE A COMMA TO SEPARATE INDEPENDENT CLAUSES JOINED BY ONE OF THE COORDINATING CONJUNCTIONS AND, BUT, OR, NOR, FOR, YET, SO.

The rains had continued for several weeks, and the garden was almost washed away.
The teacher would not accept my late essay, nor was he interested in my excuse.
I was not aware of his problem, so I could be of little help. (Avoid excessive use of so in this construction. It often suggests a juvenile style.)

NOTE: Avoid the comma splice (See Ch. 8.). If the independent clauses are not joined by a coordinating conjunction, you must use a semicolon or a period or revise the sentence.

21B USE A COMMA AFTER MOST INTRODUCTORY MODIFYING ELEMENTS: A LONG PREPOSITIONAL PHRASE, AN ADVERBIAL CLAUSE, A VERBAL PHRASE.

When I go to the market, I always buy fresh vegetables. (introductory adverbial clause)
For almost a hundred years after the fall of Vicksburg, many local citizens did not celebrate July 4. (long introductory prepositional phrase)

Swinging by his tail at the zoo, the monkey amused all of us. (introductory participial phrase)
To do well in college, one must study diligently. (introductory infinitive phrase)
By listening carefully, we were able to understand the lecture. (introductory prepositional gerundial phrase)
While walking to the store, I found a lady's purse. (introductory elliptical adverbial clause)

21C USE COMMAS TO SEPARATE ITEMS IN A SERIES AND TO SEPARATE COORDINATE ADJECTIVES.

We came to swim, to play, and to have fun.

NOTE: Most grammarians prefer a comma before the conjunction introducing the last item in a series.

The winner was an attractive, congenial young lady.

NOTE: Adjectives dealing with age are not generally separated from the preceding adjective.

Example: ugly old woman, interesting young man

21D USE COMMAS TO SET OFF NONRESTRICTIVE OR PARENTHETICAL ELEMENTS IN A SENTENCE.

NONRESTRICTIVE APPOSITIVES. If the appositive gives additional information but is not necessary for identification, set it off with commas.

The Titanic, the largest pleasure ship of its time, sank in 1912.
My sister, Eileen, has a television career. (I have only one sister.)
My sister Eileen has a television career. (There is more than one sister, so the appositive is restrictive.)

NONRESTRICTIVE PHRASES AND CLAUSES. Use a comma if the phrase or clause merely gives additional information.

Mrs. Jones, wearing the beige dress, is our secretary.
Mrs. Jones, who is wearing the beige dress, is our secretary.
BUT
The Mrs. Jones wearing the beige dress is our

secretary. (The phrase is necessary to distinguish between two or more Mrs. Joneses.)

CONTRASTED SENTENCE ELEMENTS. Use a comma to set off contrasted sentence elements introduced by not or but.

The coaching staff, not the players, was responsible for the loss.
He acted hastily, but not unwisely.

USE COMMAS TO SET OFF MATERIAL THAT IS MILDLY PARENTHETICAL OR TRANSITIONAL.

The data, although accurate, were not considered pertinent.
She knew, however, that she would not be chosen.

21E USE A COMMA TO SET OFF DIALOGUE TAGS, OR EXPLANATORY WORDS, FROM THE QUOTATION ITSELF.

She replied, "I have been waiting for an hour."
"It is not," she said, "essential that the recipient be present."

21F THE NOMINATIVE OF ADDRESS IS SET OFF BY COMMAS.

I am aware, Mr. Chairman, that I am out of order.
Gentlemen, raise the flag at the proper moment.

21G USE COMMAS CORRECTLY IN DATES, ADDRESSES, GEOGRAPHICAL LOCATIONS, AND TITLES.

She was born in Atlanta, Georgia, on May 1, 1959, in a white frame house.
John Brown, Jr., Ph.D., was graduated from Emory University on May 1, 1959, and now practices in the South.

NOTE: No commas are used when the day precedes the month:

He returned from the U.S. Navy 20 June 1984.

21H USE A COMMA AFTER THE SALUTATION AND THE COMPLIMENTARY CLOSE OF AN INFORMAL LETTER.

Dear Ethel,
Sincerely yours,

21I USE COMMAS TO SET OFF A NOMINATIVE ABSOLUTE EXPRESSION, WHEREVER IT OCCURS IN THE SENTENCE.

The day having ended, we were ready for bed.
We decided, the quarter being over, that we deserved a short vacation.

21J USE A COMMA BEFORE A FINAL PHRASE OR CLAUSE WHICH SEEMS TO PROVIDE MERELY ADDITIONAL OR PARENTHETICAL INFORMATION.

The family appreciates your kindness during the summer, especially the cards and letters which you sent.

21K USE A COMMA AFTER YES AND NO AT THE BEGINNING OF A SENTENCE.

Yes, Madam, we are aware of the problem.

21L USE COMMAS TO PROMOTE CLARITY OR TO PREVENT MISREADING, EVEN IF NO SPECIFIC RULE APPLIES.

Those who can, do; those who can't, teach.

22 SUPERFLUOUS COMMAS

Excessive and unjustified use of the comma is as disconcerting to the reader as failure to use commas where they are needed. Do not use a comma to separate the following:

1. a subject from its verb
2. a verb from its complement or object
3. compound elements joined by <u>and</u>
4. a series from the rest of the sentence
5. a preposition from its object
6. a quotation that is grammatically integrated into the sentence

The following sentences illustrate, in order, those <u>incorrect uses of the comma</u>:

1. An expert lawyer from North Carolina, defended me in the trial.
2. The art student has painted, a beautiful portrait.
3. The campaign workers finished their assignment, and mailed the letters.
4. I have always enjoyed bacon, lettuce, and tomatoes, in a sandwich.

5. The raven perched on, a bust of Pallas.
6. Television reminds us that, "a mind is a terrible thing to waste."

Name______________________________ Date_____________ Score_________

ACTIVITY 21-1, COMMA

Punctuate the following sentences correctly, using only commas and semicolons. Write C before any correct sentence.

1. Milton was blind by middle age yet he still wrote his greatest works after that time.
2. The Greek poet Homer was also blind he is acknowledged as the author of The Odyssey.
3. Alexander Pope was afflicted by spinal tuberculosis and this disease probably affected his lifestyle.
4. Voltaire was afflicted by ill health from birth however he became one of France's greatest writers.
5. Physical disability is not always a curse for it often spurs one to work against the odds.
6. Many great artists have been born with disabilities but they succeeded in spite of them.
7. Helen Keller was impaired in both sight and hearing yet she achieved great things in life.
8. Roosevelt was a victim of polio but he was elected to a fourth term as U. S. President.
9. Beethoven was almost totally deaf yet his ability as a composer is unquestioned.
10. We all have flaws of one kind or another we must try to succeed in spite of them.
11. If we win the opening game the football team will be happy.
12. While practicing last week the quarterback sprained his ankle but there were no other injuries.
13. In summer we often complain about the heat yet we are never eager to see winter arrive.
14. Because of a lengthy tour of duty he was unable to get home for his anniversary.
15. To be great is to be misunderstood.

16. After building her nest in the tree the mockingbird moved in with her mate.

17. To build a good nest takes time for it must endure the wind and the weather.

18. Lying peacefully in the hammock he enjoyed the balmy days of summer.

19. To qualify for inclusion in the volume one must be a noted scholar.

20. When preparing for an exam one should not wait until the last minute yet many students often make that mistake.

Name______________________________ Date______________ Score_________

ACTIVITY 21-2, COMMA

In the following sentences, if a comma is needed, write the word preceding it and the comma. Write C beside any correct sentence.

Example:

___*eggs,*___ I enjoy bacon, eggs and toast each morning.

________________________ 1. The Grapes of Wrath, a novel by John Steinbeck is probably his greatest work.

________________________ 2. The great works of literature, not philosophy are most readable today.

________________________ 3. After eating the children lay down to rest.

________________________ 4. In high school she studied algebra, English and two foreign languages.

________________________ 5. Life, it is said is not always a bed of roses.

________________________ 6. Shakespeare's greatest play may be the tragedy Hamlet.

________________________ 7. When I graduated from college I got a job immediately.

________________________ 8. We enjoyed the rides at the carnival especially the roller coaster.

________________________ 9. While studying my algebra I found an error in the text.

________________________ 10. Is it true that "a diamond is a girl's best friend"?

________________________ 11. This is my oldest brother whom you once met in New York.

________________________ 12. I believe that you should not go swimming immediately after eating.

________________________ 13. The unmarried person however successful, often feels unfulfilled.

______________________ 14. I was born in Atlanta, Georgia shortly after World War II.

______________________ 15. Riding next to me on the train was an ugly old man.

Name______________________________ Date______________ Score_________

ACTIVITY 21-3, COMMA

Write sentences using the following constructions, and punctuate the sentences correctly.

1. nonrestrictive appositive phrase ___________________________

____

____

2. noun in direct address _______________________________________

____

____

3. compound sentence joined by <u>for</u> ___________________________

____

____

4. two independent clauses joined by a conjunctive adverb

____

____

5. introductory adverbial clause ______________________________

____

____

6. introductory infinitive modifier ___________________________

____

____

7. nominative absolute expression _____________________________

____

____

8. coordinate adjectives modifying a noun ____________________

____

____

9. three prepositional phrases in a series ____________________

____

____

10. restrictive appositive phrase ________________________________

____

____

Name______________________________ Date_____________ Score_________

ACTIVITY 21-4, COMMA

The following sentences have only end punctuation. Insert commas as needed.

1. While in the Boy Scouts I learned to start a fire without matches to cook and to set up a tent.

2. My mother who worked for thirty years is now retired.

3. Is it true that girls not boys have superior verbal skills?

4. We are aware Mr. Jones that having made the offer you expect a quick response.

5. The father of our country George Washington had a pair of unsatisfactory wooden teeth.

6. The winding desolate road led us the members of the tour group to an antebellum mansion.

7. When the substitute teacher arrived at 8:30 my father the high school principal reprimanded him for being late.

8. Our team having won the ball game we decided that John who was the quarterback deserved an award.

9. Alexander Pope tells us that "a little learning is a dangerous thing."

10. After reading <u>The Tempest</u> one of Shakespeare's last plays boys and girls you should be able to answer my questions.

11. We do not believe however that reading one play such as <u>The Tempest</u> will make us experts in drama.

12. William after choosing his college washed his car packed his books and luggage and left home for the first time.

13. At the beginning of the quarter the bookstore had only three of the texts which the professor required.

14. When she was a contestant her knees which were usually steady were unstable shaky and impossible to control.

15. John Smith one of the oldest members of the church was married to a woman who was young energetic and pleasant.

16. William Faulkner who lived most of his life in Oxford Mississippi wrote novels short stories and poetry.

17. Swarthmore Academy our fiercest rival has lost according to the media a wide receiver a tackle and a center because of academic failure.

18. I opened the refrigerator hopefully and discovered a slice of rich creamy chocolate cake my favorite dessert.

19. While hiking last week I discovered a rare flower not one that I had seen before.

20. The ugly old man who ran the store and lived above it cheated his customers and eventually lost their patronage.

Name______________________________ Date______________ Score__________

ACTIVITY 21-5, COMMA

Insert commas as needed in the following paragraph.

Geoffrey Chaucer born in London around the year 1340 is considered one of our greatest writers especially by serious students of literature. He was a member of the commons not the aristocracy but he had friends of high birth such as John of Gaunt. In his early teens Chaucer was sent to serve in the household of a member of the nobility Prince Lionel a son of the king. Having begun his association with the nobility early in life Chaucer continued to receive the patronage of such rulers as King Edward Richard II and Henry IV. His wife Philippa who probably died in 1386 or 1387 seems not to have influenced his poetry. Although no one can be certain his experiences in France Italy and England itself seem to have made their mark. In Italy he became acquainted perhaps for the first time with the works of Dante Boccaccio and Petrarch. By the time he began work on his last major work the <u>Canterbury Tales</u> he had assimilated many literary influences especially those of France and Italy.

23 SEMICOLON

As a mark of punctuation, the semicolon is somewhat stronger than a comma and weaker than a period. It is used primarily between parts of a sentence that have the same grammatical construction.

23A USE THE SEMICOLON TO SEPARATE TWO INDEPENDENT CLAUSES NOT JOINED BY A COORDINATING CONJUNCTION.

The house was dusty and full of cobwebs; it had been vacant for several years.
Some people have worthwhile hobbies; others simply watch television.

23B USE A SEMICOLON TO SEPARATE INDEPENDENT CLAUSES JOINED BY A CONJUNCTIVE ADVERB (<u>however</u>, <u>therefore</u>, <u>consequently</u>, <u>moreover</u>, <u>otherwise</u>, <u>thus</u>, etc.) OR A TRANSITIONAL PHRASE (<u>on the other hand</u>, <u>on the contrary</u>, <u>as a result</u>, etc.).

We have put up our storm windows; therefore, we shall be ready for the chill of winter.
He did not lose the election; on the contrary, he won by a landslide.
You must keep your dogs on a leash; moreover, you need to keep your cats inside the house.

NOTE: A comma is ordinarily used after the conjunctive adverb, especially if it is more than one syllable.

23C USE A SEMICOLON TO SEPARATE INDEPENDENT CLAUSES JOINED BY A COORDINATING CONJUNCTION IF THE CLAUSES ARE LONG OR CONTAIN SUFFICIENT INTERNAL PUNCTUATION.

When I went away to college on August 29, 1965, I knew that I could get homesick; but my girlfriend, who called me each week, and my mother, who sent care packages from home, helped me adjust.

23D USE SEMICOLONS TO SEPARATE ITEMS IN A SERIES HAVING INTERNAL PUNCTUATION.

In my class in world literature it was necessary to read three major works: The Iliad, an early folk epic by Homer; The Aeneid, a literary epic by Virgil; and Dante's Inferno, Purgatorio, and Paradiso.

Name____________________________ Date_____________ Score_________

ACTIVITY 21/23 - 1, COMMAS AND SEMICOLONS

Insert commas and semicolons as needed in the following sentences.

1. We knew that rainfall was likely we did not however carry an umbrella.
2. Talent is not always enough you must also have dedication.
3. Breakfast which was served on the patio was a nutritious meal but for dinner we had vichyssoise a cold soup as the first course chicken delight which is stuffed breast of chicken and Baked Alaska for dessert.
4. Pursuing a medical degree is rigorous in fact not every-one makes it through the program.
5. The rewards of being a doctor however make the years of study seem worthwhile.
6. Taking a morning coffee break is a tradition it is there-fore a time that most employees anticipate.
7. When we choose a goal pursue it and finally achieve it we are satisfied and our parents and teachers those encouraging people behind us are proud of our success.
8. I forgot to check the oil in my old automobile as a result I had trouble on the freeway.
9. The test will take only fifty minutes then you must turn in your paper.
10. Some students spend their time wisely others however are guilty of procrastinating.

Name________________________ Date__________ Score_______

ACTIVITY 23-2, SEMICOLON

Rewrite the following sentences so that each contains two independent clauses, a semicolon, and the transitional word or phrase provided in parentheses.

1. I left my job early, and I did not get home until after 7:00 p.m. (nevertheless)

____

____

____

2. Although she tried on many dresses, she bought only a kerchief. (however)

____

____

____

3. The child had a very bad cold, so she did not attend school. (as a result)

____

____

____

4. If it were not that I just returned from my vacation, I would have been delighted to visit the national park with you. (otherwise)

____

____

____

5. The lady did not despair because of her lack of knowledge. She became eager to learn. (on the contrary)

____

____

____

6. Be prepared to wait in line for hours. Be prepared to be pushed and elbowed by those around you. (furthermore)

____

____

____

7. Some people always find something to make them happy while some always discover something to make them sad. (on the other hand)

____

____

____

8. The new mother all too often is telling her child "yes," but the new child is frequently saying "no." (in contrast)

____

____

____

24 COLON

The primary use of the colon is to introduce a list or series, explanations, and formal quotations.

24A USE A COLON TO INTRODUCE A LIST OR SERIES.

The following students will report to the principal's office: Edna, Joan, Thomas, and Martin.
Three qualities are required for this position: punctuality, integrity, and intelligence.

NOTE: Do not use a colon after forms of the verb to be when a series follows.

Wrong: The required courses are: math, history, and English.

Right: The required courses are math, history, and English.

Right: The required courses are the following: math, history, and English.

24B USE A COLON TO EMPHASIZE AN APPOSITIVE CONSTRUCTION WHICH APPEARS AT THE END OF THE SENTENCE.

American soldiers are especially proud of one charitable organization: the Salvation Army.

24C USE A COLON BETWEEN TWO INDEPENDENT CLAUSES WHEN THE SECOND CLAUSE EXPLAINS OR AMPLIFIES THE FIRST.

One thing was certain: he was not opposed to tax reform.
Everything was in order for the luncheon: the table was set, the silver was polished, and the crystal sparkled.

24D USE A COLON TO INTRODUCE A FORMAL QUOTATION ESPECIALLY ONE WITHOUT DIALOGUE TAGS.

He was reminded of Faulkner's famous words: "Man will not merely endure: he will prevail."

One of President Roosevelt's most memorable utterances appeared in a speech to the nation: "The only thing we have to fear is fear itself."

24E USE A COLON AFTER THE SALUTATION OF A FORMAL LETTER.

Dear Sir: Dear Mr. Jones:

24F USE A COLON TO SEPARATE A TITLE AND SUBTITLE, HOUR AND MINUTE FIGURES, CHAPTER AND VERSE IN BIBLICAL REFERENCE, THE ACT AND SCENE IN A PLAY.

The full title of Joseph Jastrow's book is <u>Freud: His Dream and Sex Theories</u>.
The time is now 7:14.
The minister's text for the day was John 3:16.
The quotation for us to memorize was from <u>Hamlet</u> II:2.

24G USE A COLON BEFORE A FORMAL APPOSITIVE INTRODUCED BY <u>NAMELY</u>, <u>FOR EXAMPLE</u>, <u>E.G.</u>, <u>THAT IS</u>.

The Dean suggested only one restriction: namely, that we would all observe the 10:00 curfew.

There are many fine examples of sculpture in the museum: for example, Rodin's <u>Le Penseur</u>.

NOTE: Some authorities prefer the semicolon in the construction above. However, such use violates the principle that what is on either side of the semicolon must be grammatically equal.

Name______________________________ Date_____________ Score________

ACTIVITY 24-1, COLONS

Insert colons as needed in the following sentences. Delete unnecessary punctuation.

1. At 300 p.m. the jury decided on the verdict guilty as charged.
2. In John 1, 1 we read that, "In the beginning was the Word."
3. A number of Americans have won the Nobel Prize for Literature, for example Faulkner, Hemingway, and Pearl Buck.
4. One fact is indisputable the South has produced its share of great writers.
5. A person who goes into the used car business needs to be: shrewd, personable, and energetic.
6. We always remember Polonius' famous advice to Laertes "To thine own self be true."
7. One of our required texts was <u>The Essential Self An Introduction to Literature</u>.
8. The academic counselor gave us some sound advice namely, that college was much more demanding than high school.
9. I believe that one thing is most important to the Southerner his land.
10. We went to our room at 900 p.m. and began to read the parable in Matthew 13, 3-9.

Name____________________ Date__________ Score________

ACTIVITY 21-24, REVIEW

At the point where a caret appears in the following sentences, decide whether a comma, semicolon, or colon is the best mark of punctuation. In the blank to the left write the preceding word followed by the correct mark of punctuation. If no punctuation is needed, write None.

Example:

____day;____ He remained in his room all day ^ however, he did come down for his meals.

__________ 1. There is one quality that holds a family together ^ prayer.

__________ 2. We are always told that ^ "the family that prays together stays together."

__________ 3. The teacher quoted a familiar line from the poem ^ "Gather ye rosebuds while ye may."

__________ 4. The President made one point perfectly clear ^ we must balance the federal budget.

__________ 5. There are several great epics influenced by Virgil ^ for example, Milton's Paradise Lost.

__________ 6. Your yard needs a great deal of attention ^ in fact you should hire a qualified gardener.

__________ 7. There are three important women in Wang Lung's life ^ O-lan, Lotus, and Pear Blossom.

__________ 8. The essential items that the camper requires are ^ a tent, a knife, and matches.

__________ 9. The following positions are to be filled ^ president, vice-president, and custodian.

__________ 10. There are several dangerous drugs on the street ^ namely, marijuana, heroin, and cocaine.

25 THE DASH

Use the dash sparingly and only when its use can be justified. Excessive use of the dash may result in a chatty, informal style.

25A USE THE DASH TO INDICATE A SERIOUS BREAK OR SHIFT IN THOUGHT THAT INTERRUPTS THE FLOW OF THE SENTENCE.

I saw the Abominable Snowman--my heart skips a beat when I think of it!--somewhere in the Himalayas.

If the diamond is lost--but that is not to be thought of--we are in serious trouble.

NOTE: When the material set off by dashes requires an exclamation point or question mark, it should be placed before the second dash.

25B USE A DASH AFTER A SERIES WHEN IT IS FOLLOWED BY A SUMMARIZING CLAUSE.

Rain, snow, sleet, winds--nothing stops the postman.

Teachers, students, administrators--everyone at school was affected by the strike.

NOTE: When the structure of the sentence is reversed and the series comes at the end of the sentence, a colon is generally used.

A book of verses, a loaf of bread, and you--these are the things I need to be happy.

These are the things I need to be happy: a book of verses, a loaf of bread, and you.

25C THE DASH MAY BE USED OCCASIONALLY FOR DRAMATIC EMPHASIS.

Her dress--a gaudy sequined creation--was hardly proper attire for the interview.

NOTE: In typing, distinguish between the hyphen and the dash. The dash consists of two hypens with no spacing before, after, or between.

Name______________________________ Date____________ Score__________

ACTIVITY 25-1, DASHES

Use dashes where appropriate in the following sentences.

1. I studied but who would believe it eighteen hours a day while in graduate school.
2. Life, liberty, and the pursuit of happiness these are guaranteed in the Constitution.
3. He answered, "I would advise you to but you aren't even listening."
4. The storm by now it had become a hurricane had winds of 120 miles per hour.
5. The beach house at least it had once been a beach house was leveled by the force of the winds.
6. A family, a home, and a job these are what most of us need for true happiness.
7. Nothing and I cannot emphasize this too strongly can prevent me from getting revenge.
8. This piece of glass I found it in my grandmother's attic, you know is now highly collectible.
9. I next mentioned the dream theories of Freud do you know his work and the audience quickly perked up.
10. Wine, women, and song all had robbed him of his wealth.

Rewrite the following sentences, making use of dashes to indicate a shift in thought, to provide dramatic emphasis, or to conclude a series which precedes a summarizing clause.

1. I tore my dress, but I don't know how, while I was at the reception.

____

____

____

2. Neither rain, nor sleet, nor snow, nor any inclement weather prevents the postman from his duty.

3. I reached into my pocket for my wallet, and, my gosh, it was gone.

4. The young boxer, although he didn't have a chance of winning the match, stepped into the ring.

5. The children, the parents, even the grandparents help to repair the city after the flood.

26-29 PERIOD, EXCLAMATION POINT, QUESTION MARK, QUOTATION MARKS

26 PERIOD

There are three end marks of punctuation: period, question mark, and exclamation point. All of them, however, may also be used within a sentence.

26A USE A PERIOD AT THE END OF A DECLARATIVE SENTENCE.

Nothing is certain but death and taxes.

26B USE A PERIOD, NOT A QUESTION MARK, AT THE END OF AN INDIRECT QUESTION.

He asked me if I intended to mow the lawn.
She wanted to know what we were planning to do with the estate.

26C USE A PERIOD AFTER MOST ABBREVIATIONS AND INITIALS.

B.C. A.D. Ms. Dr. Co. Ph.D.

The period is not ordinarily used in abbreviations of government agencies and company names. Acronyms do not require periods.

FBI CIA IBM WAVES CORE

26D USE A PERIOD AS A DECIMAL POINT.

.98 2.173 $.25 $2843.82

27 EXCLAMATION POINT

The exclamation point, used to express strong emotion, should be used sparingly. It may occur after an interjection or at the end of a sentence.

Hurrah! Our team finally won a game.
Get out of my house immediately!
"Get out of my house now!" she yelled.

28 QUESTION MARK

The question mark signals a direct question and usually appears at the end of a sentence. It may, however, be used internally.

28A USE THE QUESTION MARK AFTER A DIRECT QUESTION.

Why do you think he failed to show up?
"Why do you think," she said, "he failed to show up?"
Will he fail? be demoted? be forced to resign?

28B USE THE QUESTION MARK WITHIN PARENTHESES TO INDICATE UNCERTAINTY. DO NOT, HOWEVER, USE IT AS A RESULT OF LAZINESS IN RESEARCH.

Aristophanes was born in 446 B.C. (?) in Athens.

28C USE A QUESTION MARK WITHIN SENTENCES AS NEEDED.

Pablo Picasso--you know his work, don't you?--is a major figure in twentieth-century art.

29 QUOTATION MARKS

Quotation marks are used primarily to enclose the exact words of a written or spoken source.

29A ENCLOSE DIRECT QUOTATIONS IN QUOTATION MARKS.

She replied, "I'll think about that tomorrow."
"I wonder," she mused, "if he will return to us."
According to Sir Francis Bacon, "Wives are young men's mistresses, companions for middle age, and old men's nurses."

29B USE QUOTATION MARKS WITH DIALOGUE, AND INDENT PROPERLY.

When the speaker in dialogue changes, a new paragraph begins.

"Do you have a suspect in the murder case?" asked the captain.

"No," replied the lieutenant, "not yet."

"Well, keep working on it."

29C USE SINGLE QUOTATION MARKS TO INDICATE A QUOTATION WITHIN A QUOTATION.

"Did the professor say," Joan asked, "that we must read `A Rose for Emily' this week?"
"When Hamlet says to Ophelia, 'Get thee to a nunnery,' he may be playing with words," replied the scholar.

29D USE CORRECTLY OTHER MARKS OF PUNCTUATION WITH QUOTATION MARKS.

The comma and the period always go inside the quotation marks. The colon and the semicolon always go outside. The question mark and the exclamation point may go inside or outside the quotation marks, depending on the construction.

Examples:

For tomorrow we must read "Ode on Melancholy."

"For tomorrow," he said, "you must read 'Ode on Melancholy.'"
"Did the teacher say," I asked, "that we must read `Ode on Melancholy'?"
He firmly stated, "Your grade will be based on your test scores"; then he left the room.

29E USE QUOTATION MARKS TO ENCLOSE TITLES OF MOST POEMS, SHORT STORIES, ARTICLES, SHORT MUSICAL WORKS, AND SPECIFIC EPISODES WITHIN A REGULAR RADIO OR TELEVISION SERIES. THE LONGER WORK IN WHICH THE SHORTER ONE APPEARS IS USUALLY ITALICIZED.

Shelley's "Ode to the West Wind" has a number of memorable lines.
One of my favorite compositions is Chopin's "Minute Waltz."
The teacher read to us selections from Emerson's famous essay "Self-Reliance."

NOTE: The Bible is not italicized, and books of the Bible are not put in quotation marks.

29F USE QUOTATION MARKS WITH WORDS USED IN A SPECIAL SENSE, WITH INVENTED WORDS, AND WITH WORDS WHICH SUGGEST A DIFFERENT LEVEL OF USAGE.

Her one meal of the day, at mid-afternoon, she called "lupper."
Elizabeth-Jane annoyed her father by suggesting that she had been "hag-rid."

29G THE DEFINITION OF A WORD, ESPECIALLY WHEN IT COMES FROM A DICTIONARY, IS OFTEN ENCLOSED IN QUOTATION MARKS.

The word defenestrate means "to throw (something or someone) out of a window."

Name______________________________ Date______________ Score_________

ACTIVITY 26/29-1, PERIOD, EXCLAMATION POINT, QUESTION MARK, QUOTATION MARKS

Insert punctuation as needed in the following sentences.

1. Have you read, she asked, My Last Duchess, a dramatic monologue by Browning
2. No, I replied, but I have often read Tennyson's Ulysses
3. I wonder if poetry is really worth reading?
4. Damn the torpedoes shouted one hero of the U.S. Navy.
5. The article entitled Love in the Afternoon was highly romantic.
6. Does the dictionary say that the Latin prefix <u>ab</u> means down from or away from
7. Fire Fire yelled the usher in the theater.
8. Do you intend to fight to resign to give up
9. When will you find the time, my mother asked, to read Faulkner's Dry September
10. Old Mademoiselle Reisz--you remember her, don't you--played Chopin's Impromptu for her guest.

Write five sentences using the punctuation indicated.

11. (quotation marks with exclamation point)

____

____

____

12. (quotation marks with semicolon)

____

____

____

13. (quotation marks with commas)

____

____

____

14. (question mark inside quotation marks)

____

____

____

15. (question mark outside quotation marks)

____

____

____

30/31 SLASH AND ELLIPSES

30 SLASH

The slash, often called the diagonal, is an uncommon punctuation mark.

30A USE THE SLASH TO DIVIDE LINES OF POETRY THAT ARE NOT OTHERWISE SEPARATED FROM YOUR OWN WRITING.

These lines in T. S. Eliot's "Prufrock" may suggest modern superficiality: "In the room the women come and go / Talking of Michelangelo."

Notice the space before and after the slash.

30B USE THE SLASH TO EXPRESS FRACTIONS THAT ARE NOT WRITTEN OUT.

three-fourths 3/4 one-half 1/2

30C USE THE SLASH SPARINGLY TO EXPRESS A CHOICE BETWEEN TWO TERMS.

and/or his/her

31 ELLIPSES

The sign of the ellipsis is three spaced periods to indicate omission. There is a space before and after each period.

31A USE AN ELLIPSIS TO INDICATE THAT YOU ARE OMITTING MATERIAL IN A QUOTATION.

Original

> "No man is an island, entire of itself; every man is a piece of the continent, a part of the main."

As it might appear in your paper

> John Donne suggests in Meditation XVII that "No man is an island . . . ; every man is a . . . part of the main."

If the ellipsis occurs at the end of the sentence, four periods will be required.

31B USE THE ELLIPSIS TO INDICATE THAT A SENTENCE TRAILS OFF OR IS LEFT UNFINISHED.

"Sometimes," he muttered to himself, "I wonder if . . . ."

NOTE: This usage is confined primarily to informal writing.

32/33 BRACKETS AND PARENTHESES

32 BRACKETS

For brackets, which are not to be confused with parentheses, there are two uses: to enclose your own editorial interpolation within a quotation and to enclose parenthetical matter within material already in parentheses.

32A USE BRACKETS TO ENCLOSE EDITORIAL INTERPOLATIONS.

According to the local paper, "The recent hurricane [Elena] has caused millions of dollars in damage to the Gulf Coast."

Sir Francis Bacon advises us wisely in his essay "Of Studies": "Reading maketh a <u>full</u> man, conference a <u>ready</u> man, and writing an <u>exact</u> man [italics mine]."

32B USE BRACKETS AROUND THE LATIN WORD SIC TO INDICATE AN ERROR IN THE QUOTATION IN GRAMMAR, SPELLING, ETC.

The Ku Klux Klan, " said the orator, "does not believe in intergration [sic]."

NOTE: The word <u>sic</u> is no longer underlined in the quotation and is not followed by a period.

32C USE BRACKETS TO ENCLOSE PARENTHETICAL MATTER WITHIN PARENTHESES.

The anthropologist then decided (or so she said in her second book [1982]) that her former conclusions about the natives had been hastily made.

NOTE: This is obviously an awkward use of brackets and should be avoided whenever possible.

33 PARENTHESES

Like the dash, parentheses show an interruption in the flow of the sentence, but they indicate that the material they enclose is less important than the remainder of the sentence. Parentheses are more emphatic than the comma.

33A USE PARENTHESES TO SET OFF LOOSELY RELATED EXPLANATORY MATERIAL WITHIN A SENTENCE.

This bottle of wine (I was assured of its character) is from a California vineyard.

Muscadines and scuppernongs (they are surely ripe by now) produce delicious jellies.

33B USE PARENTHESES TO ENCLOSE DIRECTIONS AND REFERENCES.

The Middle Ages (see the Introduction) was a period of social upheaval in England.

In formal writing, avoid use of slang or colloquialisms. (See Ch. 40.)

33D USE PARENTHESES TO ENCLOSE NUMERICAL FIGURES REPEATED FOR ACCURACY.

The charge for the new roof will be nine hundred dollars ($900.00).

The faculty senate will consist of seven (7) members from the Division of Liberal Arts.

33D USE PARENTHESES TO NUMBER ITEMS IN A LIST.

Please remember to follow this procedure: (1) fill in the application completely; (2) take it to our main office; (3) talk with the Director of Personnel; (4) leave a number where you can be reached.

33E USE PARENTHESES CORRECTLY WITH OTHER MARKS OF PUNCTUATION.

Within a sentence the parenthesis will rarely be preceded by a punctuation mark. The end mark of punctuation will go outside the parenthesis.

> The intern observed the surgery (it was his first time in the operating room) and promptly fainted.

> If you should lose your way (and that is entirely possible), call me for directions.

Although parentheses and dashes are to some degree interchangeable, parentheses are more common when the parenthetical material is a complete sentence.

If the parenthetical material is not part of another sentence, the period goes inside the closing parenthesis.

> Faculty members will teach one class off campus. (This does not apply to part-time instructors.)

Name______________________________ Date______________ Score_________

ACTIVITY 32/33 - 1, BRACKETS AND PARENTHESES

In the following sentences, decide whether brackets or parentheses should be used where the caret (∧) appears. In the blank to the left write the word Brackets or Parentheses.

______________________ 1. According to the western newspaper, "The calvary ∧ sic ∧ appeared in the nick of time."

______________________ 2. The college charges twenty dollars ∧ $20.00 ∧ per quarter hour.

______________________ 3. This wife of mine ∧ I married her ten years ago ∧ has turned into a veritable shrew.

______________________ 4. The nominative case ∧ see Chapter 28 ∧ is used as the subject of a finite verb.

______________________ 5. The measurements of the tomb ∧ 20 by 20 feet ∧ were considered significant by the archaeologist.

______________________ 6. "This well-known play ∧ Suddenly Last Summer ∧ has the quality and effect of Greek tragedy," says one critic.

______________________ 7. The biology text ∧ I referred to it earlier ∧ has an interesting chapter on genetics.

______________________ 8. Always avoid the fused sentence and comma splice. ∧ Refer to Section 8. ∧

______________________ 9. Your mortgage payment will be ninety-five dollars ∧ $95.00 ∧ .

______________________ 10. The Scarlet Letter appeared in the nineteenth century ∧ 1850 ∧ and secured Hawthorne's reputation.

Name________________________________ Date_____________ Score__________

ACTIVITY 21-33, REVIEW

This exercise covers all preceding marks of punctuation. Punctuate each sentence correctly, and be prepared to justify your choice. Delete unnecessary punctuation.

1. "What did he mean she asked when he said you will pay for this
2. One thing is absolutely certain Mr. Smith our present senator will not be re-elected.
3. I wonder, if we should report the accident to the police?
4. Reading, writing, and studying grammar these are the fundamentals of college English courses.
5. "Get out of my life you beast forever she screamed
6. The following speakers will make a presentation at the convention on October 25 1985 Reese Colton Atlanta Georgia Libby Smith Tampa Florida and Bill Bates Birmingham Alabama.
7. If you arrive before 830 p m you may use the key under the doormat.
8. What do you think class she asked of Washington Irving's short story Rip Van Winkle
9. Emerson informs us that, "to be great is to be misunderstood
10. After I graduated from college on June 1 1965 I entered graduate school but when after four years of study I received my terminal degree I still could not get a job.
11. American teenagers especially those living along the coast are primarily interested in one activity surfing
12. When I was given a copy of the Bible for Christmas I immediately began to read from the first chapter of Isaiah.
13. The information in interviewing techniques see Chapter 3 is essential reading for all employers.

14. The elderly teacher she must have been at least seventy had no wish to retire.

15. Adam and Eve had only one restriction namely not to eat of the Tree of Knowledge.

16. When it snows in southern Georgia quite a rare occurrence the children are ecstatic.

17. Wine she said should be sipped and savored not gulped down

18. The children all have measles they have not however been confined to bed.

19. Her three children John Joseph and Joshua came to spend the summer however they stayed until Christmas.

20. Sexual activity she said is on the rise among today's teenagers who come from wealthy homes

34 APOSTROPHE

The apostrophe is used to show possession, to form the plurals of letters, figures, and some words, and to indicate contractions.

34A USE THE APOSTROPHE AND S TO FORM THE POSSESSIVE CASE OF MOST SINGULAR NOUNS.

man's job, boy's clothes, child's lunch

NOTE: The possessive case of singular nouns ending in s may be formed by adding only the apostrophe or the apostrophe and s. Add only an apostrophe if the addition of s causes difficulty in pronunciation.

Keats' or Keats's, James' or James's
Mr. Jones' house or Mr. Jones's house
for Jesus' sake, Demosthenes' orations

34B USE ONLY THE APOSTROPHE TO FORM THE POSSESSIVE OF PLURAL NOUNS ENDING IN S.

dogs', boys', girls', ladies'

If the plural noun does not end in s, add the apostrophe and s to form the possessive.

men's, women's, children's

34C USE THE APOSTROPHE WITH THE LAST WORD TO SHOW JOINT POSSESSION.

Smith and Peabody's General Store
Sam and John's room
but: Sam's and John's rooms (separate ownership)

34D ADD THE APOSTROPHE TO THE LAST PART OF A COMPOUND PHRASE TO SHOW POSSESSION.

my mother-in-law's nagging
my sister-in-law's house
my sisters-in-law's houses (plural)
everyone else's opinion

34E DO NOT USE THE APOSTROPHE TO FORM THE POSSESSIVE CASE OF PERSONAL PRONOUNS.

hers, yours, theirs, ours
but: everyone's nobody's, someone's

34F USE THE APOSTROPHE IN CONTRACTIONS TO SHOW THAT A LETTER OR LETTERS HAVE BEEN OMITTED.

don't, won't, can't, haven't

34G USE THE APOSTROPHE AND S TO FORM THE PLURAL OF WORDS REFERRED TO AS SUCH, LETTERS, FIGURES, AND ABBREVIATIONS.

You have too many <u>and's</u> and <u>but's</u> in your sentences.

Be sure to distinguish between your <u>i's</u> and <u>e's</u>.

In elementary school I had difficulty making <u>2's</u> and <u>8's</u>.

M.F.A.'s and Ph.D.'s are considered terminal degrees.

34H USE THE APOSTROPHE ONLY WHEN IT IS NEEDED.

1. Do not use the apostrophe to form the possessive of most nouns denoting inanimate objects.

    No: the desk's top
    Yes: the top of the desk

No: the house's paint
Yes: the paint on the house
Yes: the bottom of the barrel
Yes: the baby's bottom

NOTE: Exceptions established by usage include a _day's_ work, an _hour's_ time, a _moment's_ delay, etc.

2. Do not confuse _it's_ and _its_.

   _It's_ time we left for school.

   The dog had lost _its_ tail.

Name______________________________ Date_____________ Scale_________

ACTIVITY 34-1, APOSTROPHE

Add apostrophes as needed in the following sentences. Write C in front of any correct sentence.

1. Mary and Joans locker was in the womens section of the gymnasium.
2. Your continental *7*s look too much like our American *F*s.
3. Youre joking when you say that the award is hers, arent you?
4. Whos going to decide whose book it is?
5. Robert Burns poetry is required reading in his class and hers, but not in everyone elses.
6. Its true that B.A.s generally require four years intensive study.
7. The writing may be yours, but the ideas are hers.
8. Its no longer certain that a mans home is his castle.
9. Girls dresses and ladies lingerie are on sale at Felton and Smiths department store.
10. One of the proofreaders jobs was to cross all *t*s and dot all *i*s.
11. Theyre not attending this weeks classes.
12. The three students papers all began with identical sentences.
13. I never know whats on his sisters mind.
14. The cafeterias meals usually make use of yesterdays food.
15. My daughters friends cant speak for a minute without adding *ands* after every statement.
16. James book has six missing pages.
17. Shes not very tall, but a persons height isnt everything.

18. Theirs are the books on the upper shelf.

19. My advice is to delete whats irrelevant and retain all thats significant.

20. There are so many M.D.s in our city that this years phone book added two pages.

Name____________________________ Date_____________ Score_________

ACTIVITY 34-2, APOSTROPHE

In the blanks at the right, give the singular possessive and the plural possessive of each word.

Example: girl	*girl's*	*girls'*
1. mouse		
2. goose		
3. child		
4. Jones		
5. sheep		
6. freshman		
7. country		
8. son-in-law		
9. ox		
10. baby		
11. American		
12. niece		
13. store		
14. brother		
15. day		
16. paper clip		
17. pest		
18. boss		
19. executive		
20. Anglo		
21. dictionary		

22. monkey ____________ ____________

23. state ____________ ____________

24. communist ____________ ____________

25. lottery ____________ ____________

26. mapmaker ____________ ____________

27. major general ____________ ____________

28. press association____________ ____________

29. Seventh-day Adventist____________ ____________

30. vertebra ____________ ____________

35 HYPHEN

The hyphen is a device in mechanics indicating to the reader that two words or two parts of a single word belong together. The hyphen should not be confused with the dash.

35A USE THE HYPHEN TO CONNECT THE PARTS OF A COMPOUND WORD. Always consult the dictionary when in doubt.

1. Between two parts of a compound adjective preceding the noun it modifies: a well-educated teacher, a well-seasoned skillet, an ill-tempered man

NOTE: This rule does not apply to ly words which are adverbs: a highly skilled professional.

Compound adjectives that follow the verb and serve as subjective complements are usually not hyphenated.

The essay was well written.
The man was ill tempered.

2. Between the parts of compound numbers from twenty-one through ninety-nine

3. Between parts of a fraction: one-fourth, two-fifths

4. Between parts of compound nouns, verbs, and adverbs that are always hyphenated: self-abasement, great-grandson

35B USE A HYPHEN TO AVOID AMBIGUITY OR A CONFUSING COMBINATION OF LETTERS.

He had to re-collect the raffle tickets that had been given away.
He recollected that there had once been a house at this location.
A steel-like material was being used.

35C USE A HYPHEN PROPERLY WITH TWO OR MORE SEPARATED MODIFIERS OF A SINGLE WORD.

A fifteen- to twenty-page paper is required.
Both pre- and post-bellum skirmishes were noted by the historian.

35D USE A HYPHEN FOR PROPER SYLLABICATION AT THE END OF A LINE.

The man in the glass-bottom boat is character-
istic of tourists who come to Florida.

Do not divide a word of one syllable: through, asked, strength, rhythm.

Do not place a single letter at the beginning or the end of a line, and do not place a two-letter ending of a word at the beginning of a line.

Incorrect: ox-en, a-void, original-ly

Name________________________________ Date______________ Score__________

ACTIVITY 35-1, HYPHENS

In the following sentences, if a word should be hyphenated, write that word hyphenated correctly in the blank to the left. Write C for any correct sentence.

______________________ 1. Winning the game was an experience never to be forgotten.

______________________ 2. I was congratulated on having a well organized presentation.

______________________ 3. The instructions are self explanatory.

______________________ 4. This letter requires a twenty-two cent stamp.

______________________ 5. On campus students must pay an activities fee.

______________________ 6. Students who live off campus, however, are exempt.

______________________ 7. He felt that twentieth century fiction was often overrated.

______________________ 8. Was the information that you collected well received?

______________________ 9. She has always been known as a self indulgent person.

______________________ 10. His pseudo sophistication was evident to everyone.

Listed below are pairs of compound words. Make correct use of one of the pair in a sentence which you compose.

1. (sugar coated, sugar-coated)

____

____

____

2. (a ne'er-do-well, a ne'er do well)

3. (sulphur dioxide, sulphur-dioxide)

4. (cloven hoofed, cloven-hoofed)

5. (a ghost town, a ghost-town)

36 UNDERLINING (ITALICS)

Material that is underlined in typed or handwritten copy is set in italic print in the printed copy.

36A USE ITALICS FOR THE TITLES OF NEWSPAPERS, MAGAZINES, PLAYS, LONG POEMS, BOOKS, COURT CASES, LONG MUSICAL COMPOSITIONS, AND WORKS OF ART.

The New York Times is a comprehensive daily paper. (Underline the name of the city only if it is part of the name of the newspaper.)

We spent the entire quarter reading Milton's *Paradise Lost*.

Handel's *Messiah* is performed every Christmas.

Van Gogh's *Sunflowers* is one of the period's most popular paintings.

36B USE ITALICS FOR THE NAMES OF SHIPS, TRAINS, PLANES.

Have you ever traveled on the *Southern Crescent*?

We viewed *The Spirit of St. Louis* at the museum.

The explosion of the *Hindenburg* was an unexpected disaster.

NOTE: Do not italicize abbreviations such as H.M.S. and U.S.S. before the names of ships.

36C USE ITALICS SPARINGLY FOR EMPHASIS.

Are you *positive* that you can identify the killer?

I wanted to know *where*, not *when*.

36D USE ITALICS TO INDICATE FOREIGN WORDS OR PHRASES THAT HAVE NOT BEEN TOTALLY ASSIMILATED INTO THE ENGLISH LANGUAGE.

It is considered *de rigueur* to wear hat and gloves to Sunday services.

This poem is representative of the *carpe diem* school of literature.

You cannot enjoy a traditional Christmas without the mistletoe (*Phoradendron flavescens*) as decoration.

36E USE ITALICS TO INDICATE WORDS, LETTERS, OR NUMBERS REFERRED TO AS SUCH.

The word *receive* is often misspelled in freshman compositions.

You must distinguish between *i's* and *e's* in your writing.

The *3's* and *8's* were often confusing to the accountant.

Two Greek letters are the source of our word *alphabet*.

Name______________________________ Date_____________ Score_________

ACTIVITY 36-1, UNDERLINING (ITALICS)

If a sentence is correct, write C in the blank at the left. If not, write in the blank the word, letter, etc. that should be italicized.

Example:

abalone	How do you pronounce abalone?
____________	1. We were supposed to read Coriolanus, one of Shakespeare's less popular plays.
____________	2. Don't forget to cross your t's in this paragraph.
____________	3. The section entitled "An Awakening" in Anderson's Winesburg, Ohio is one of my favorites.
____________	4. For our annual cruise we have booked passage on the H.M.S. Royal Princess.
____________	5. The word avert comes from a Latin root meaning "to turn away."
____________	6. There are several rings around the planet Saturn.
____________	7. After he sprained his ankle, he was hors de combat for two weeks.
____________	8. Is it true that Michelangelo's Pieta was once damaged by a madman?
____________	9. The magnolia (Magnolia grandiflora) is the state flower of Mississippi.
____________	10. The author spent twenty years doing research for his magnum opus.
____________	11. How many and's appear in his sentence?
____________	12. The Latin term for one type of false reasoning is post hoc ergo propter hoc.

_______________ 13. I said money, not many!

_______________ 14. The best source for synonyms is Roget's Thesaurus.

_______________ 15. One Middle English word that has survived in our modern language is that.

Name______________________________ Date______________ Score__________

ACTIVITY 36-2, ITALICS

Write sentences containing the following, and italicize correctly.

1. title of a book and a chapter

____

____

2. a foreign word or phrase

____

____

3. a word referred to as such

____

____

4. the name of a ship

____

____

5. a word used for emphasis

____

____

6. a number referred to as such

____

____

7. title of a novel by Hemingway

____

____

8. title of a long musical composition by Beethoven

9. title of a court case

10. a letter in the alphabet referred to as such

37 CAPITALIZATION

37A USE A CAPITAL LETTER FOR THE FIRST WORD IN A SENTENCE AND THE FIRST WORD IN A DIRECT QUOTATION.

Now is the time for us to show courage.
The Dean of Students asked, "Are you planning to live in the dormitory?"

Do not capitalize the first word of a direct quotation that has been grammatically integrated into the sentence.

The police department reports "a measurable increase in the number of burglaries."

Capitalize the first word of each line of poetry.

Let me not to the marriage of true minds
Admit impediments. Love is not love . . . .

37B CAPITALIZE PROPER NOUNS AND WORDS DERIVED FROM PROPER NOUNS.

England
English
Colombia
Colombian coffee
the Sahara
Felder St.
St. Lawrence River

Do not capitalize proper nouns or adjectives which have become established as common. Consult your dictionary.

China	my sister from Cologne
a set of china	a bottle of cologne

37C CAPITALIZE THE NAMES OF GEOGRAPHICAL LOCATIONS.

North South East Midwest

Do not use capitals when referring to directions.

Drive south three miles before turning east.

37D DO NOT CAPITALIZE THE NAMES OF THE SEASONS UNLESS THEY ARE PERSONIFIED.

During the winter he lived in the South.
Old Winter is shaking his icy locks.

37E CAPITALIZE NAMES OF NATIONALITIES, RACES, AND ETHNIC GROUPS.

Negro, Negroid, Italian, Polish, Acadian

Black and White may be capitalized or not, but consistency is required. If one is capitalized, the other should be also.

37F CAPITALIZE NAMES INDICATING RELIGIOUS GROUPS, DENOMINATIONS, BOOKS, EVENTS, AND THE DEITY.

The Shakers are a rapidly dwindling group.
Yom Kippur is a holy day for the Jews.
The date of Easter may vary annually.

NOTE: Pronouns referring to the Deity may or may not be capitalized.

37G USE CAPITAL LETTERS WITH SUCH SCHOOL-RELATED ITEMS AS LANGUAGES, NUMBERED COURSES, ACADEMIC DEGREES (WITH NAMES), AND THEIR ABBREVIATIONS.

The applicant has an M.A. from Cornell and a Ph.D. from Princeton.

I am taking French, History 101, sociology, art, and American literature.

Capitalize academic degrees only after a name.

37H CAPITALIZE THOSE TITLES PRECEDING A NAME, TITLES OF HIGH RANK OR POSITION, AND TITLES WHICH SUBSTITUTE FOR PARTICULAR NAMES.

President Reagan	Her Majesty
the President	Mr., Mrs., Ms. Jones
Queen Elizabeth	Aunt Ida

Words indicating family members are not capitalized unless they substitute for the name or accompany the name.

I went to New York with Mother and Father to visit my uncle.
My grandfather lives with Aunt Ethel.

37I CAPITALIZE IMPORTANT WORDS IN THE TITLES OF PUBLICATIONS SUCH AS BOOKS, NEWSPAPERS, PERIODICALS. Capitalize the first word or letter in a subtitle.

The name of our text is <u>Prose Style: A Handbook for Writers</u>.
<u>The Ox-Bow Incident</u> is required reading.

NOTE: Both elements in a hyphenated word in the title are capitalized.

37J ALWAYS CAPITALIZE THE PRONOUN <u>I</u> AND THE EXCLAMATION <u>O</u>.

"Repent, O ye sinners, before it's too late," I urged from the pulpit.

37K CAPITALIZE IMPORTANT WORDS IN THE SALUTATION BUT ONLY THE FIRST WORD IN THE CLOSING OF A LETTER.

My dear Jonathan,	Sincerely yours,
Dear Friends,	

Name______________________________ Date______________ Score_________

ACTIVITY 37-1, CAPITALIZATION

Write a capital letter above each letter that should be capitalized. Use parentheses ( ) to indicate that capitalization is optional.

1. The newest senator in the u.s. senate was formerly a representative from louisiana.
2. Although spring comes early in the south, summer takes its place very shortly.
3. "Do you think," she said, "that farmers in the midwest are in economic difficulty?"
4. She ate brussel sprouts and french fries for lunch and drank colombian coffee afterwards.
5. Both the whites and the blacks in my class are attentive, but the oriental student from taiwan seems especially interested.
6. My teacher, who is from a small town in vermont, received his bachelor's degree from m.i.t.
7. I go to visit grandfather each winter because he lives in the south; my grandmother still prefers to live alone in the north.
8. He was a democrat by family ties, but he joined the republican party in 1980.
9. Every good christian should know that good friday precedes easter sunday.
10. The title of his new text is <u>Arthur: a study in heroism</u>.

Name______________________________ Date_____________ Score_________

ACTIVITY 37-2, CAPITALIZATION

Insert capital letters above the lower case letters as needed in the following paragraphs.

Publius vergilius maro is the full name of the latin writer now known simply as virgil or vergil. he was born in andes, a small village near the city of mantua, in 70 b.c. Virgil probably studied in the cities of cremona, milan, and naples. The curriculum included philosophy, rhetoric, science, and literature.

Some years later virgil became the friend of octavius, the roman emperor known to history as augustus caesar. You may remember him from the book of Luke in the bible. it is said that he sent out a decree "that all the world should be taxed." At any rate, octavius became the friend and patron of Virgil and encouraged him to write an epic of the roman people. This literary epic he worked on for the rest of his life. it was called the <u>aeneid</u> from its hero aeneas, who had escaped his homeland after the trojan war. Although the work was relatively complete, virgil was still not quite satisfied with it when he died on september 21, 19 b.c. after a trip across the Adriatic sea.

The <u>aeneid</u> was made ready for publication by virgil's literary executors. It now stands in the company of such great epics as homer's <u>iliad</u> and <u>odyssey</u> and Milton's <u>Paradise lost</u>.

38 ABBREVIATIONS AND NUMBERS

Abbreviations are merely short cuts which writers often use. Some have become standard in formal writing. The general rules for abbreviations are summarized here.

38A THE FOLLOWING ABBREVIATIONS ARE ALWAYS ACCEPTABLE.

Before a name:
Ms. Wilson, Mr. Smith, Messrs., Mmes., Mt., Rev. (only with the full name, as in the Rev. John Doe)

After a name:
Degrees, such as M.D., Ph.D., and Jr., Sr., Washington, D.C.

Times and dates
49 B.C., 11:00 p.m.

Institutions, companies, agencies, etc.
NEA AFL-CIO Prentice-Hall, Inc.

Bibliographic references and footnotes
Ibid., pp., vol., ed., cf.

38B SPELL OUT NUMBERS THAT START SENTENCES, OR RECAST THE SENTENCE.

Three hundred and thirty-five freshmen have applied for admission.

The registrar indicates that 335 freshmen have applied for admission.

38C SPELL OUT ROUND NUMBERS THAT CAN BE EXPRESSED IN ONE OR TWO WORDS. USE ARABIC NUMERALS OTHERWISE.

twenty-seven	2713
one thousand dollars	$1,173.13
one-half	3 1/4

38D USE FIGURES FOR NUMBERS WHEN THERE ARE SEVERAL IN A SENTENCE OR PARAGRAPH.

The athletes had varying body styles. One weighed 100 pounds, another tipped the scales at 285 pounds, several were average at 175 pounds, and one actually weighed well over 300.

38E THE FOLLOWING FORMS ARE ACCEPTABLE FOR DATES, PAGE NUMBERS, STREET NUMBERS, PERCENTAGES, AND HOURS OF THE DAY.

June 14, 1789
the third of June or 3 June 1975
Look at page 30 in your text.
Room 12 is now vacant.
I live at 803 South Lee; I once lived at 3 South Main.
During the 1970's he received 17 per cent interest on his investments.
The rehearsal ended at 10 P.M. (or 10:00 p.m.)
The rehearsal ended at ten o'clock (with <u>o'clock</u> the number is spelled out).

Name________________________________ Date______________ Score__________

ACTIVITY 38-1, ABBREVIATIONS AND NUMBERS

Write the numbers in the following sentences correctly, and correct any errors in abbreviation. Make your corrections above the error.

1. John Reeves, Doctor of Veterinary Medicine, has been treating a bull that weighs three hundred and twenty-seven lbs.
2. His office opens at 8 o'clock and closes at six P.M.
3. The meeting will be held at the branch office located at 125 3rd Avenue.
4. Rev. Jones will pronounce the benediction at approximately 9 o'clock.
5. According to our western civ teacher, the Roman empire fell Anno Domini four seventy-six.
6. 2712 people applied for the fellowships, but only 1213 received them.
7. John Hays, Junior, the first son of John Hays, Senior, plans to name his child John Hays the Third.
8. In the year 1980 people were buying houses at an eighteen and a half per cent interest rate.
9. Go to room two hundred twelve on the 2nd floor and look on page twenty-five of the unabridged dictionary.
10. Three hundred and thirteen students live in the residence hall located at One Hundred One Wheatley St.

39 SPELLING

The rules that have been established for correct spelling are numerous. Some of them are helpful; most of them are easy to forget. The advice that every writer should follow is threefold: pronounce correctly, memorize the correct spelling, and consult the dictionary when in doubt. The following section gives only a summary of the most important spelling rules.

39A PLURALS

1. Most nouns form their plural by adding -s to the singular.

   hair, hairs,   cat, cats   girl, girls

2. Nouns which end in ch, x, z, sh, and s usually form their plural by adding es.

church, churches	box, boxes	gash, gashes
lunch, lunches	ax, axes	lash, lashes

3. If a noun ends in y preceded by a consonant, change the y to i and add es.

lady, ladies	memory, memories
fantasy, fantasies	ability, abilities
frailty, frailties	liberty, liberties

4. Nouns that end in ey, oy, ay form their plurals by adding s.

monkey, monkeys
turkey, turkeys
buoy, buoys
donkey, donkeys

5. Nouns ending in o preceded by a consonant usually add es.

tomato, tomatoes
potato, potatoes
hero, heroes
torpedo, torpedoes

6. Most musical terms ending in o and nouns ending in o preceded by a vowel add merely s.

alto, altos
soprano, sopranos
impresario, impresarios
radio, radios

7. Compound or hyphenated nouns usually add s to the significant word in the compound.

mother-in-law, mothers-in-law
lady in waiting, ladies in waiting
court martial, courts martial

8. The plurals of foreign nouns must be memorized.

criterion, criteria
synopsis, synopses
medium, media
alumnus, alumni
alumna, alumnae
datum, data

NOTE: A number of foreign words have acceptable English plurals. Consult a dictionary.

39B WORDS WHICH CONTAIN THE COMBINATION IE OR EI

Use i before e
Except after c
Or when sounded as a
As in neighbor and weigh

receive
conceive
believe
relief
grief
eight

Notable exceptions are weird, seize, seizure, their.

39C WORDS ENDING IN E

Most words ending in silent e drop the e before a suffix beginning with a vowel.

desire	desiring, desirable
share	sharing
resemble	resembling, resemblance
appropriate	appropriating

Words ending in a silent e usually keep the e before a suffix beginning with a consonant.

hope	hopefully
sincere	sincerely
appropriate	appropriately
require	requirement

NOTE: Words ending in ce or ge usually retain the e when a suffix follows if the pronunciation requires it.

change	changeable
notice	noticeable
advantage	advantageous

39D WORDS ENDING IN Y

Change y to i before all suffixes except ing. This rule does not apply to plurals.

beauty	beautiful
happy	happiness
study	studying
try	trying

Name______________________________ Date______________ Score_________

ACTIVITY 39-1, SPELLING

In the blank at the right, enter a C if the sentence is correct. If there is an error, give the correct form of the misspelled word.

1. The accident allegedly occured on February 13, 1981. __________________________
2. If you did not receive the check, perhaps it has been accidentially misplaced. __________________________
3. While picking the tomatoes, I was bitten by several mosquitos. __________________________
4. Some radios nowadays have mechanisms which prevent interferance by other stations. __________________________
5. Do you remember the noticable increase in mumps that occurred last year? __________________________
6. He failed the test because he had not been doing enough studing. __________________________
7. The topazes in these rings are conspicuously large. __________________________
8. After picnicing in the den, we had to vacuum the carpet. __________________________
9. The derelict was buried in the local cemetary by our priest. __________________________

10. I was dissatisfied with his diagnosis of my illness as diptheria. ______________________

11. We ate in a dinning area that had a beautiful hanging chandelier. ______________________

12. We baked two turkies and invited aunts and uncles, nieces and nephews. ______________________

Name______________________________ Date______________ Score_________

ACTIVITY 39-2, SPELLING

Many spelling errors are made because of words that look or sound alike. Underline the correct word in parentheses in the sentences below.

1. The passage you have (sited, cited, sighted) from Shakespeare is not a familiar one.
2. Everyone (except, accept) George decided to decline your invitation.
3. The incident to which he (alluded, eluded) is known to the police.
4. An (eminent, imminent) official in the church will christen the child.
5. The dome on the (capital, capitol) is decorated with gold from Georgia.
6. The prisoner (affected, effected) his escape from jail by using a rope ladder.
7. The tailor will (altar, alter) my suit for the ceremony.
8. A cup of (coarsely, coursely) chopped walnuts is to be used in the recipe.
9. The (principal, principle) he always followed was total honesty.
10. She is now retired, but she was (formally, formerly) an ambassador to Ireland.
11. I was so (scared, scarred) by the English teacher that I dropped the course.
12. Lucifer was the brightest of the fallen (angles, angels).

13. My grandfather, who lived through the Depression, (hoards, hordes) food all year long.

14. Very few politicians are ever (censored, censured) by the U.S. Senate.

15. She had lost her child in the (isles, aisles) of the supermarket.

16. My interest in skiing (past, passed) after I broke my leg.

17. A carpet will often crawl if it is not made (stationary, stationery).

18. Were you familiar with the (anecdote, antidote) with which he opened his speech?

19. As valedictorian, you are to (precede, proceed) me in the graduation line.

20. How does my performance (affect, effect) the audience?

Name________________________ Date____________ Score__________

ACTIVITY 39-3, SPELLING

In the blank to the right, write the plural of each of the following nouns. If more than one form is acceptable, write both of them.

1. gypsy ________________________
2. tornado ________________________
3. sympathy ________________________
4. alumnus ________________________
5. medium ________________________
6. curriculum ________________________
7. goose ________________________
8. sheep ________________________
9. mouse ________________________
10. talisman ________________________
11. son-in-law ________________________
12. Mr. ________________________
13. Mrs. ________________________
14. synopsis ________________________
15. echo ________________________
16. piano ________________________
17. dwarf ________________________
18. grouse ________________________
19. bus ________________________
20. fly ________________________
21. turkey ________________________

22. alto ______________________

23. fish ______________________

24. chairman ______________________

25. gynecologist ______________________

26. sergeant-at-arms ______________________

27. sequence ______________________

28. separatist ______________________

29. family ______________________

30. elf ______________________

Name______________________________ Date_____________ Score__________

ACTIVITY 39-4, SPELLING

In the following sentences strike through the incorrectly spelled word or words and write the correct spelling above.

1. You have accidently mispelled three words in this paragraph.
2. If you have a greivance to discuss with the perfessor, you should make an appointment.
3. She received hardy congradulations after her wedding in Febuary.
4. The goverment has gone to grate lengths to improve our enviroment.
5. We should all realize that participating in atheletics is no substitute for studing.
6. Each canidate must basicly be responsible for his own re-election.
7. The duel exhausts on his car were the soul reason for his trouble with the police.
8. Be especialy carefull not to loose your way in these dark allies.
9. We were priviledged to recieve council from such an imminent politician.
10. The cruise on the yacht was truely one to remember.

40 THE DICTIONARY

A hardcover collegiate dictionary is an indispensable part of college study. In addition to providing definitions, a good dictionary indicates proper spelling, pronunciation, and syllabification. A collegiate dictionary also provides information regarding parts of speech, word forms, etymology, and usage; often, the dictionary offers synonyms and antonyms.

40A USE STANDARD ENGLISH IN COLLEGE WRITING.

College writing should make use of standard English: that is, a form of English which is understood by a broad group of English speakers. Words that carry a special meaning for a particular group of people often are unclear to a broad audience. The following dictionary labels suggest that a term or a meaning is not standard among English speakers: Nonstandard, Informal, Slang, Regional, Dialectal, Chiefly British, Archaic, Obsolete.

Note on Slang

> Slang is comprised of words and phrases that are fashionable for a relatively short period of time among a particular group of people--often young people. Depending on the generation, a person who

dressed or acted according to the latest fashions would be considered "the cat's pajamas," "a cool daddy-o," "hip," "far-out," "in," or "boss." The problem with slang is that the special meaning it has usually fades very quickly. What remains is a rather silly phrase. Avoid slang in formal writing.

40B BE AWARE OF DENOTATIONS AND CONNOTATIONS OF WORDS.

The denotation of a word is its explicit meaning--the literal meaning provided in a dictionary. The connotation of a word is a suggested meaning beyond its literal one. These suggested meanings can be negative (freeloader as opposed to charity recipient). They can also be positive (freedom fighter as opposed to terrorist). A writer must realize that the connotation of a word can either support or undercut the intended meaning of the material.

NOTE: Problems with connotations sometimes occur when the writer makes use of synonyms. Synonyms are words which have the same or nearly the same meaning. Many synonymous words, however, have different connotations. Thus, a writer should consider the connotation as well as the denotation of any synonym used.

40C USE PROPER IDIOMS.

An idiom is a form of expression that belongs to a particular language. No one really "catches" a bus in the sense of capturing a bus. Nevertheless, "to catch a bus" is proper idiomatic English. Those idiomatic expressions which give the most problems are usually those including prepositions.

agree to (a proposal)	different from (not than)
agree with (a person)	identical with (not as)
bring about (a change)	plan to (not on)
bring up (a point)	succeed in (not to)
concerned with (a project)	sure to (not and)
concerned about (a problem)	try to (not and)

Name______________________________ Date____________ Score__________

ACTIVITY 40-1, THE DICTIONARY

Identify the following dictionary abbreviations. Note: The introductory material of the dictionary typically clarifies abbreviations and labels.

Example: *OE* *Old English*

1. *vi.* ______________________________
2. *vt.* ______________________________
3. *adj.* ______________________________
4. *n.pl.* ______________________________
5. *Gk.* ______________________________
6. *Lat.* ______________________________
7. *biol.* ______________________________
8. *obs.* ______________________________
9. *Fr.* ______________________________
10. *naut.* ______________________________
11. *dial.* ______________________________
12. *adv.* ______________________________
13. *syn.* ______________________________
14. *ant.* ______________________________
15. *ME* ______________________________

Using a dictionary, indicate the etymology of each of the following words. Note: Identify both original language and root meaning.

Example: avuncular *Latin: avunculus, maternal uncle*

16. aphrodisiac ______________________________
17. ayatollah ______________________________
18. cosmopolitan ______________________________

19. devious ____________________

20. devour ____________________

21. gerrymander ____________________

22. heptagon ____________________

23. hickory ____________________

24. intramural ____________________

25. journey ____________________

26. kamikazi ____________________

27. lexicon ____________________

28. manufacture ____________________

29. noise ____________________

30. Yellow journalism ____________________

Name______________________________ Date_____________ Score________

ACTIVITY 40-2, THE DICTIONARY

In most recent collegiate dictionaries, the following words will be followed by a label. Indicate the label attached to each word and the definition to which the label is attached.

Example: argufy: *Regional - to argue over*

1. irregardless: ______________________________
2. brae: ______________________________
3. jerk: ______________________________
4. zinger: ______________________________
5. slob: ______________________________
6. snafu: ______________________________
7. meatball: ______________________________
8. nosy: ______________________________
9. nanny: ______________________________
10. nerd: ______________________________
11. deja vu: ______________________________
12. nouveau riche: ______________________________
13. novena: ______________________________
14. zeitgeist: ______________________________
15. zilch: ______________________________
16. geek: ______________________________
17. doghouse: ______________________________
18. dumb: ______________________________
19. pink: ______________________________
20. rumble: ______________________________

21. ruddy: ______________________________

22. hack: ______________________________

23. gig: ______________________________

24. tin can: ______________________________

25. redeye: ______________________________

26. loop: ______________________________

27. mosquito boat: ______________________________

28. parallel: ______________________________

29. static: ______________________________

30. truss: ______________________________

Name________________________________ Date______________ Score__________

ACTIVITY 40-3, THE DICTIONARY

Each pair of words has roughly the same denotative meaning. With the aid of a dictionary, provide definitions which indicate the different connotations.

Example: transient (*adj.*) *one passing through from one place to another.*

vagrant (*adj.*) *a public nuisance without a home.*

1. childish (*adj.*) ____________________

   childlike (*adj.*) ____________________

2. feminine (*adj.*) ____________________

   effeminate (*adj.*) ____________________

3. loving (*adj.*) ____________________

   amorous (*adj.*) ____________________

4. request (*v.*) ____________________

   plead (*v.*) ____________________

5. modest (*adj.*) ____________________

   prudish (*adj.*) ____________________

6. generous (*adj.*) ____________________

   prodigal (*adj.*) ____________________

7. agreeable (*adj.*) ____________________

   pliant (*adj.*) ____________________

8. humorous (*adj.*) ____________________

   foolish (*adj.*) ____________________

9. evaluate (*v.*) ____________________

   criticize (*v.*) ____________________

10. investigation (*n.*) ____________________

    inquisition (*n.*) ____________________

11. satisfy *(v.)* ____________________

glut *(v.)* ____________________

12. pious *(adj.)* ____________________

sanctimonious *(adj.)* ____________________

13. saliva *(n.)* ____________________

spit *(n.)* ____________________

14. noble *(adj.)* ____________________

arrogant *(adj.)* ____________________

15. omission *(n.)* ____________________

error *(n.)* ____________________

16. observe *(v.)* ____________________

ogle *(v.)* ____________________

17. blemish *(v.)* ____________________

mutilate *(v.)* ____________________

18. misappropriate *(v.)* ____________________

steal *(v.)* ____________________

19. courage *(n.)* ____________________

nerve *(n.)* ____________________

20. nightgown *(n.)* ____________________

negligee *(n.)* ____________________

41 EFFECTIVE LANGUAGE

For a piece of writing to be effective, it should include general as well as specific statements. It may present abstract concepts but should also make use of concrete details.

41A USE SPECIFIC LANGUAGE TO SUPPORT GENERAL STATEMENTS.

Unsupported generality

> The book was quite readable.

Revised with support

> The many examples, the frequent illustrations, and the straightforward language made the book quite readable.

Unsupported generalities

> Many careers are quite exciting. Others can be very lucrative. Some careers may involve years of schooling while others require on-the-job training.

Revised with support

> Many careers that a college graduate might choose are quite exciting. A physical education major, for example, can become a cruise ship activity director. As part of her job, she would travel for nine months a year to such places as the Virgin Islands, Jamaica, and Acapulco, not to mention Miami and New York. Such a career, however, may not be as lucrative as that of a stock broker. A successful broker may sell 50,000 shares of stock on a given day, making upwards of $1000 commission daily and as much as $250,000 a year. A stock broker's position demands on-the-job training that may last three to six months. Other careers--that of a medical doctor, for example--involve four to five years of schooling after college as well as an internship of one to three years.

41B USE CONCRETE LANGUAGE TO SUPPORT ABSTRACT CONCEPTS.

Unsupported abstractions

> My father insisted on fairness.
>
> Rampant anger can result in misery.

Revised with support

> My father insisted on fairness even to the extent that he would not read one of us children a story without also doing something special for the other.
>
> If our anger over such a thing as not being invited to a party causes us to be curt with all those around us, we may soon find ourselves with no invitations and with no friends to speak to.

41C USE LANGUAGE SUITED TO COLLEGE WRITING.

Pretentious, jargon-filled, or cliché-ridden language can be as inappropriate as slang when writing in an educational or professional context. The use of archaic words--words that are no longer in current usage--may seem to add formality but tend only to obfuscate the writing. Neologisms--words that are recently created--may seem to enliven writing but often only obstruct clarity. Jargon--specialized terminology belonging to a particular profession--can make writing incomprehensible to a general audience. Pretentious or inflated language is sometimes used to impress a teacher, but it usually results in awkward and wordy sentences.

41D AVOID WORDINESS.

Never say with five words what can be said clearly with three. If appropriate, choose the active voice, which is less wordy than the passive voice.

Wordy	Succinct
last but not least	finally
at this point in time	now
in this day and time	now
due to the fact that	because

Passive Voice

The book was read by most of the students.

Active Voice

Most students read the book.

Needless repetition

While sometimes effective for emphasis, repetition often results in imprecise writing. Repetition of a concept using different words usually results in redundancy.

Repetitions

His greatest problem was his temper, for his temper was sometimes uncontrollable.

I knew the senator, but I did not know the senator's wife.

Revision

His greatest problem was his temper, which was sometimes uncontrollable.

I knew the senator but not his wife.

Redundant

return back to	unique and one of a kind
my own personal	revert back
the basic essentials	advanced planning

41E AVOID CLICHÉS.

Some phrases, although once original, are now so overused that they have lost true meaning. They are instead kinds of mass-manufactured thoughts which lazy thinkers borrow as substitutes for original ideas. For example, rather than give a careful analysis of a person's qualities, one might simply provide a cliché--"She is as honest as the day is long."

Clichés

knowing full well	the straight and narrow
better late than never	sink or swim
better safe than sorry	truer words were never spoken
crazy like a fox	nipped in the bud

Name______________________________ Date_____________ Score_________

ACTIVITY 41-1, EFFECTIVE LANGUAGE

The following sentences may contain language that is inflated, archaic, newly created, jargon-filled, and cliché ridden. Draw a line through inappropriate words or phrases and provide an effective substitute.

Example: Britain ~~never had its act together~~ *was politically disorganized* and had a difficult time resisting ~~xenos~~ *foreign invaders*.

1. Britain received its insular shape during the Ice Age as a result of large glaciations.
2. The glaciations showly melted and, presto, the island of Britain appeared as big as day.
3. With reference to invaders, Britain has had a hard time of it throughout history.
4. It has experienced myriad ingressors.
5. An early group of invaders who really shook things up were the one and only Romans.
6. You can bet that the Romans easily beat up the couple of tribes that tried to resist.
7. The locals caused few problems for the cracker jack Roman troops, but the cream soon rose to the top.
8. It was the main man, Julius Caesar, who cleped the country Britannia.
9. Because of the civilizing input of the Romans, Britain had new interstates.
10. The new Roman towns were like condo-cities when compared to the pup-tents of the outlanders.

11. In the ensuing interregnum following the Roman decampment, Britain was invaded by Nordic warriors.
12. The Nordic tribes bullied the Britains for about two centuries before the invaders broke their spirits.
13. The invading tribes created a mess, but following the initial welter, a heptarchy established itself.
14. In the seventh century, one of the seven kingdoms took the lead and society was okay until Britain was conquered by the Normans.
15. The political situation stunk during the Norman conquest, but every cloud has a silver lining and Britain generally prospered under succeeding rulers.

Name________________________________Date________________ Score________

ACTIVITY 41-2, EFFECTIVE LANGUAGE

Draw a line through any unnecessarily wordy phrases in the following paragraph. If a new phrase is necessary, provide a concise substitute.

Many of the people of the great nation of the United States have distant and ancient ancestors who, it seems, lived in the country of Britain. This country of Britain has a long history and a very interesting history, in my opinion. At some time in the past around the year 55 B.C., Julius Caesar traveled from Rome with his troops and legions and caught up with some tribes of Britain, who were attacked by him. Britain was attacked by Julius Caesar once and then again. After the country was attacked and invaded, then the country was named Britannia by Julius Caesar. Due to the fact that the Roman soldiers and troops were far and away better fighters in terms of organization, Britain was able to be occupied by Romans around about the year of 47 A.D. to about 400 A.D., the year of our Lord. On account of the Roman invasion of Britain, the country of Britain had at this early point in time some towns which were built after the style of Roman towns, and the country of Britain also in addition was the recipient from the Romans of a network of roads and highways made of stone. At the current day and time, some highways and roads in Britain still as yet follow the early roads previously made and built earlier by the Roman people.

Name________________________________ Date______________ Score_________

ACTIVITY 41-3, EFFECTIVE LANGUAGE

For each of the following general or abstract phrases provide sepcific, concrete supporting materials in the form of a modifying phrase or clause.

Example: an odd teacher *who had a wart on his nose and a tendency to cough after every sentence.*

1. an antagonistic person________________________________
____
2. an unfortunate circumstance____________________________
____
3. political freedom____________________________________
____
4. a reputable mechanic_________________________________
____
5. a stupid movie_______________________________________
____
6. difficult homework____________________________________
____
7. a strange student_____________________________________
____
8. an unbelievable concert_______________________________
____
9. a strenuous program___________________________________
____
10. an adventurous summer_________________________________
____

Name_________________________ Date____________ Score_________

ACTIVITY 41-4, EFFECTIVE LANGUAGE

Write down five clichés that you have heard. Below each cliché write an original way of expressing the general idea contained in the cliché. NOTE: Do not make use of any of the clichés presented in Section 41e.

1a. Cliché: ____

1b. Revision: ______________________________________

2a. Cliché: ____

2b. Revision: ______________________________________

3a. Cliché: ____

3b. Revision: ______________________________________

4a. Cliché: ____

4b. Revision: ______________________________________

5a. Cliché: ____

5b. Revision: ______________________________________

Write down five euphemistic phrases. Below each euphemism, write a straightforward statement of the idea expressed in the euphemism.

6a. Euphemism: _____________________________________

6b. Meaning: _______________________________________

7a. Euphemism: _____________________________________

7b. Meaning: _______________________________________

8a. Euphemism: _____________________________________

8b. Meaning: _______________________________________

9a. Euphemism: ____

9b. Meaning: ____

10a. Euphemism: ____

10b. Meaning: ____

42 FIGURATIVE LANGUAGE

Writers can make use of similes, metaphors, personification, and other figures of speech to enliven their compositions.

42A USE METAPHORS AND SIMILES TO STRENGTHEN WRITING.

Comparisons, when judiciously used, can clarify the point being made and add vividness to the writer's language. Metaphors and similes both make comparisons. A metaphor is, in fact, an implied comparison; for example, the statement my head is exploding contains the metaphor exploding which implicitly compares a discomfort, probably a headache, to the action of explosives. A simile is an explicit comparison which usually makes use of the terms like or as, as in she is as stubborn as an old goat. In this simile, the comparison between the woman and the goat is stated, not merely implied as in the metaphor. Both metaphors and similes can be effective in clarifying points and enlivening language.

42B USE PERSONIFICATIONS, OVERSTATEMENTS, AND UNDERSTATEMENTS TO ADD FRESHNESS TO WRITING.

If used sparingly, personification can add originality and interest to a piece of writing. Personification is a kind of writing which gives human traits to animals, inanimate objects, and ideas. Note the personification in this sentence: He attempted to sleep, but small anxieties over the loss of his job would sneak into his subconscious and disturb his restfulness. Here, through the use of the words small, sneak, and disturb, anxieties are given qualities not unlike those of mischievous children. By providing human qualities to ideas or things, personifications can make a piece of writing more interesting.

Overstatement and understatement, if used infrequently, can effectively draw attention to a particular passage.

Overstatement is a conscious exaggeration.

> The fitness instructor proceeded to reduce us to a blob of clay and then rebuild us into Greek gods.

Understatement is a deliberate deemphasis.

> For a trained runner, a refreshing afternoon jaunt of twenty miles may take a mere two hours.

42C AVOID EXCESSIVE USE OF EXPRESSIVE LANGUAGE.

The frequent use of such words as always, never, greatest, best, worst makes statements unbelievable. There are very few instances in which a statement is always or never true. In addition, overuse of such words as really, very, truly, actually, as well as words such as fabulous, incredible, awesome, exciting, and wonderful makes for tedious reading. Rather than add drama or emphasis, these overused words usually appear to the reader as no more than wearisome filler.

Indeed, the overuse of one or a combination of figures of speech can make writing wordy and pretentious.

Name______________________________ Date______________ Score_________

ACTIVITY 42-1, FIGURATIVE LANGUAGE

Provide an original simile that effectively describes or characterizes each of the following.

Example: Even in a crisis, my father is as calm *as an experienced doctor in the midst of surgery.*

1. She was nervous about her first speech______________________

____

____

2. All too often, when drinking and driving are involved, teenagers die____

____

____

3. Neglected old people often grow weary with living_________

____

____

4. Drugs can invade a person's body and mind________________

____

____

5. The day before a term paper is due, students scurry around the library____

____

____

Add freshness and emphasis to the following sentences by rewriting them, making use of overstatement or understatement.

Example: The first year of college is filled with new experiences.

The first year of college battered my senses with a thousand new experiences and a million new ideas.

6. Missing the final exam was unwise. ______

7. She spent a long time preparing her term paper. ______

8. His handwriting was not very clear. ______

9. He failed four out of five courses. ______

10. She liked to talk in the student center. ______

Name______________________________ Date____________ Score__________

ACTIVITY 42-2, FIGURATIVE LANGUAGE

Draw a line through figurative language that seems excessive and replace it with a more suitable expression. If the language is appropriate, write a <u>C</u> to the left of the sentence.

Example: In the 1960's ~~Ares, the god of war, pulled the Goliath~~ *the large nation of* America *entered* into conflict with the *tiny country of* ~~Lilliputian~~ Vietnam.

1. The most controversial and bloodiest war in American history was the Vietnam War.
2. The war was fought in another world under conditions that were somewhat less than satisfactory.
3. An entire generation of young Americans were exposed to experiences which left everyone with permanent emotional scars.
4. Although the war was light years away, U.S. citizens had instantaneous reports of battles through the news media.
5. Television, a messenger of ill tidings, brought grim reports of the war into our homes.
6. Every American cried as he witnessed the most brutal of war atrocities.
7. It seemed that no one--whether American or Vietnamese--was spared from war's cruelty.
8. All of Mother Nature in Vietnam was ruined by the fiery hands of bombs.
9. The war dragged on, like an aged woman, for an eternity.

10. Finally, the dove of peace descended upon the land and there was, for a short time, an end to the killing.

43 EFFECTIVE PARAGRAPHS

A paragraph consists of a number of sentences focusing on a single topic. The paragraph is a basic component of many larger compositions, such as the essay, the research paper, and the report.

PARAGRAPH STRUCTURE

A paragraph may be "built," sentence upon sentence, in several ways. A common structure makes use of a topic sentence and supporting material. In this case, the topic being discussed is introduced in one of the first sentences. This topic sentence is followed by facts, details, examples, or statements made by authorities on the topic. This specific material supports or verifies the statement made in the topic sentence.

Another structure reverses the order of the above-mentioned method and employs a number of supporting statements that culminate in the statement of the topic. Here, specific facts, examples, etc. logically lead to the final statement of the topic.

Occasionally, the topic is not stated but clearly implied through the statements in the paragraph. In most of these instances, the reader can easily express the general topic statement implied in the writing.

43A PARAGRAPHS MUST BE COHERENT.

Coherence is present when the material of the

paragraph has an understandable order and when there is a logical relationship among the various statements in the paragraph. Coherence can be produced if the paragraph is developed according to a predetermined order.

Time order. A paragraph making use of a chronological, or time, order presents events in the sequence in which they happened, beginning with the first and proceeding onward.

Position order. A paragraph using the position, or spatial, order presents details or images in a particular way to enhance understanding. A physical description of an object--a dormitory room, for example--might begin with the floor and proceed step by step to the ceiling. On the other hand, the description may present seemingly unconnected images from various parts of the room in an attempt to capture a sense of the room's disorder.

Order of importance. A paragraph using the climactic order, or order of importance, presents ideas, statements, or examples in such a way that the reader senses a pattern of development. The paragraph may progress from the least important to the most important point, or it may sandwich weaker ideas between stronger ones. Ideas may also be organized so that a problem is first presented, then a resolution, or so that an occurrence is presented, then its effect.

Deduction. Although it is actually a reasoning process, deduction also provides a basis for ordering a paragraph. As a method of organization, the deductive process can be thought of as beginning with a general statement which is then applied to a specific situation.

General	No student likes to get overcharged for pizza. Bill is a typical student.
Specific	He recently went to Joe's Pizza and found that he paid more for pizza than at Fred's or Mary's or any other pizza place in town. It is a good bet that Bill did not like spending the extra money and will not go to Joe's again.

Induction. The inductive process makes use of specific information to formulate a general conclusion. As a method of organization, the inductive process can be thought of as beginning with a series of specific incidents or observations which are then used as a basis for a general statement.

Specific	I get little sleep on Sunday evening, so I wake up tired on Mondays. I always miss breakfast, and I am usually late for my first class. If I have a Monday test, I mostly am unprepared and usually do not do well. <u>All in all</u>,
General	<u>Mondays are not good days for me</u>.

43B USE TRANSITIONAL PHRASES TO IMPROVE PARAGRAPHS.

A <u>transitional</u> phrase provides a link or a bridge between ideas that may not seem clearly related.

WITHOUT TRANSITION:	I ran in a 10-kilometer race. I slept well. I was sore.
REVISED WITH TRANSITIONAL PHRASE:	I ran in a 10-kilometer race. <u>That night</u>, I slept well. <u>However</u>, the next morning I was sore.

Transitional words and phrases

Addition: additionally, again, also, and, besides, furthermore, in addition, moreover, so too

Comparison: in comparison, in the same way, likewise, similarly

Concession: admittedly, although, granted, while it is true

Contrast: although, but, however, in contrast, on the other hand

Examples: for example, for instance, in fact, in particular, specifically.

Summary: in all, in conclusion, in short, in summary, to conclude

Time: after, at first, currently, in the past, meanwhile, next, then

43C DEVELOP EFFECTIVE INTRODUCTIONS TO CREATE INTEREST.

An effective introduction evokes the reader's interest while providing him with an understanding of both the topic and the perspective from which it is to be viewed. Certain strategies can provide for interesting introductions. The following are examples of possible paragraph beginnings.

Contrast or reversal

Most know what makes a good college; few discuss those qualities which belong to a bad college.

Definition

Many people argue for or against welfare, yet few know what welfare actually is.

Description

A recent wreck that I witnessed made me fully aware of the hazards of drinking and driving.

Dramatic incident

Jorge, a seven-year-old immigrant child, had a first day of school that was like no one else's.

Historical background

The drafting of eighteen year olds into the army has its roots in wars as far back as the Revolution.

Problem

The recent trend toward specialization in education has confronted businesses with a surprising problem: they lack well-rounded and well-read junior executives.

Refutation

Perhaps the most widely held misconception in America is that foreign language study is useless.

NOTE: Avoid introductions that do not focus on a topic, or that call attention to you as a writer or to the writing process.

43D PROVIDE A GOOD CONCLUSION.

A good conclusion provides a completion for the various points and arguments made in your paper. It is not simply the end of your writing; it is the logical culmination of all that you have presented. The following statements exemplify certain strategies which are useful in conclusions.

Call for action

As indicated, there are numerous and complex reasons for voter apathy. However, there is one simple solution: vote in the next election!

Review of main points

The harmful effects on physical health, the debilitating effects on mental achievement, the stultifying effect on social activity--all clearly indicate that drugs are best avoided.

Deduction

If one accepts the original premise that America historically has been enriched by immigrants, then the data regarding economic, cultural, and political benefits make it clear that America should not close its borders.

Prediction

The legalization of euthanasia could combine with the currently legalized abortion to provide a vehicle for culling out the imperfect and infirm. Thus, euthanasia takes us one step closer to a "Big Brother" society.

NOTE: Avoid conclusions that are tedious summaries of the paper's main points, or that call attention to you or the writing process. Avoid conclusions that espouse moral lessons or, worse, close with aphorisms or clichés. Definitely avoid conclusions that introduce new subjects or new supporting material.

Name______________________________ Date_____________ Score_________

ACTIVITY 43-1, EFFECTIVE PARAGRAPHS

Provide a list of facts or details that support each of the following topics. Order your material according to the method indicated.

1. A person's first day at college is unforgettable. (time order)

   A.

   B.

   C.

   D.

   E.

2. A college library is a valuable information source if a person knows what a library has to offer. (position order)

   A.

   B.

   C.

   D.

   E.

3. A student will survive in college only if she organizes her activities according to certain priorities. (order of importance)

   A.

B.

C.

D.

E.

4. Not everyone who begins college will receive a degree. (deduction)

   A.

   B.

   C.

   D.

   E.

5. There is a definite process involved in preparing for an examination. (time order)

   A.

   B.

   C.

   D.

   E.

Name______________________________ Date______________ Score_________

ACTIVITY 43-2, EFFECTIVE PARAGRAPHS

Add appropriate transitional phrases in the following paragraph. Make use of those discussed in this chapter as well as others which you know.

A research paper is not difficult if a student knows when to begin and how to go about his project. _____________________ it is important that the student determine a clear topic to be researched. _____________________ he should narrow the topic and determine a specific point which he will clarify or an issue which he will resolve. _____________________ a conscientious student will read as much as he can related to his topic. _____________________ most students read very little. _____________________ they later find themselves with little to say about their topics. While reading, a student should take careful notes on points which are important to his research. _____________________ he should begin outlining his paper and preparing a rough draft. Material learned from reading should be incorporated into the paper. _____________________ it must be carefully noted, or the student will be guilty of plagiarism. _____________________ the paper is revised, and from this process a finished paper emerges. _____________________ if a student conscientiously follows these procedures outlined, he will produce better research papers and better grades.

Name______________________________ Date____________ Score__________

ACTIVITY 43-3, EFFECTIVE PARAGRAPHS

Write an introduction of several sentences making use of the following topics. Rely on the methods for writing introductions discussed in this chapter.

1. Terrorism

____

____

____

____

____

2. Alcoholism

____

____

____

____

____

3. Student Activity Fees

____

____

____

____

____

4. College Athletics

____

____

5. Student Financial Aid

Name____________________________ Date____________ Score_________

ACTIVITY 43-4, EFFECTIVE PARAGRAPHS

Write two paragraphs, one presenting a general topic statement followed by specific material, the other presenting specific material followed by a general topic statement. For both paragraphs, use the pieces of information provided below. However, provide an original general topic statement.

> Wide ties were popular in the 50's and 70's.
> Narrow ties were popular in the 60's and 80's.
> Short hair, fashionable with our grandfathers, is fashionable again.
> Button-down shirts were old-fashioned 10 years ago, and now they are stylish.
> Hats, which have not been popular for 30 years, are even making a comeback.

Paragraph #1

General Statement: ____

____

____

Specifics: ____

____

____

____

____

____

____

____

____

____

____

____

Paragraph #2

Specifics: ____

____

____

____

____

____

____

____

____

____

____

____

____

General Statement: ____

____

____

44/45 REASONING: EVIDENCE AND VALID ARGUMENTS

Sound Evidence

Facts, examples, and authorities together comprise the information--the evidence--upon which a writer builds his paper and bases his conclusion. In one sense, a writer is like a lawyer. The writer presents his case and his evidence to the reader, who decides if the writer's assertions are reasonable and acceptable. Finally, the reader judges the evidence which the writer presents.

Facts, statistics, the results of surveys and experiments--these things are primary evidence and often are most convincing to a reader.

Citations from books presenting the conclusions of authorities, and direct quotations of these authorities--these things are secondary evidence and also offer strong support for your ideas.

44A USE EVIDENCE THOUGHTFULLY AND CAREFULLY.

Ask the following questions when gathering evidence.

Does the evidence weigh in favor of one or another point of view? (If the evidence does not favor your viewpoint, it may be that you wish to change your viewpoint.)

Are the sources of evidence reliable and respected? (Make use of professional journals, encyclopedias, and reputable newspapers and magazines.)

Is my information timely and relevant? (Your evidence is worthless if a more recent study proves it false. It is also worthless--no matter how interesting it seems--if it does not directly relate to your topic.)

What do my statistics say? (Be certain that your statistics are presented in such a way that they are understandable. Be certain that your interpretation of the statistics is reasonable.)

Is my analysis of the evidence impartial? (Do not ignore the conclusion that the evidence points to just because you do not like that particular conclusion. Research has little place for personal preference.)

Is my so-called evidence actually made up of opinions, assumptions, and inferences? (An opinion, no matter how widely held, remains an opinion and needs actual evidence to support its validity. Do not provide opinions or assumptions to support your viewpoint unless you present the evidence underlying those assumptions.)

Valid Arguments

To be convincing, a paper must be reasonable. If a reader determines that there is an error in the reasoning used in a paper, that reader may reject all of the information and ideas in the paper, however true they are. Make use of sound reasoning, and guard against errors.

45A ELIMINATE ERRORS IN REASONING.

Avoid unsupported generalizations. A general statement, whether or not it is true, is relatively worthless unless it is supported with specific evidence. Furthermore, the evidence must be adequate to support the statement. One example of a crime does not support the view that a city offers poor police protection. Limit statements as much as feasible and offer ample evidence supporting the general statements.

Avoid selecting only data supporting your viewpoint. Stacking the evidence so that only your side is heard may at first appear convincing. However, once the reader realizes that you are withholding the truth, he will reject your paper.

Avoid emotional appeals. A sad story can be found to suit almost any circumstance, and intelligent readers are aware of this fact. Some readers realize that your presentation of a sad story may be a way of revealing that you have few sound reasons for your viewpoint.

Avoid popular appeals. Reading is an intellectual process. Few readers will be convinced to change their judgment because your view is part of "the American way," because "everyone believes this to be true," or because your view can be supported by some other popular slogan.

Avoid post hoc reasoning. Post hoc ergo propter hoc literally means "after this, therefore because of this." This faulty line of reasoning suggests that if one thing happens after another, then one must be caused by the other. In reality it may be that there is no connection between the two events. Consider: "I ate a bowl of ice cream last night and woke up this morning with an upset stomach. It must have been the ice cream." Is there no other possible cause?

Avoid attacking the person rather than the idea. It seems easy to reject a person's idea because the person has some conspicuous flaw. However, the writer's task is to judge ideas, not the people who make the ideas.

Avoid inappropriate or biased authorities. An authority is very knowledgeable of his field but may know little or nothing about other fields of knowledge. It makes no more sense to quote tennis players as authorities on insurance than it does to quote insurance salesmen as authorities on tennis. Also, some actual authorities may be biased in their views. An expert engineer, for example, will not likely present a view that would damage the company for which he works. His bias will be toward his company.

Avoid begging the question. A writer who begs the question assumes that the question, or issue to be proved, is in fact true. Instead of presenting evidence in support of a viewpoint, this writer offers as evidence a restatement of the viewpoint. Consider:

> Jim is a man of honesty and intelligence because he is both virtuous and wise.

Avoid sidetracking the reader with false issues. It is possible that one may avoid the real issue by concentrating on a minor related issue. Providing convincing evidence on a minor point, however, does not necessarily prove the major point to be true. For example, a person may, in fact, prove that the power company overcharged him on his last bill. That does not, however, prove that the power company is run by organized crime.

Avoid polarizing an issue. It may be that there are many alternatives to one viewpoint. It is improper to tell the reader that there are only two, either this one or a clearly impractical one. Either/or and all-or-nothing reasoning usually is based on oversimplifying an issue and involves flawed reasoning.

Avoid arguments that do not follow logically from the evidence. A non sequitur (it does not follow) is a statement that does not logically derive from the evidence. Consider: The fact that the last two Presidents of this country have been unable to solve our financial problems proves that socialism would be a better political alternative. Does it necessarily follow that a country with economic problems is best served by socialism? Has the writer provided any evidence to support his claim?

Name______________________________ Date_____________ Score_________

ACTIVITY 44-1, EFFECTIVE EVIDENCE

The following statements include evidence which is either sound or unsound. Determine whether the evidence is effective in supporting the opinion set forth. If the evidence is effective, place an E before the sentence. If the evidence is biased, irrelevant, opinionated, etc. and thus unsound, place an X before the sentence.

_____ 1. Since 70% of the students in my advanced art class favor governmental support of artists, it is fair to say that most Americans would support public support for artists.

_____ 2. Children are getting smarter. A study conducted in 1963 revealed a continual increase in student aptitude as measured by the S.A.T. test.

_____ 3. Our armed forces are not receiving adequate funding. This fact was stated by the United States Secretary of Defense in a recent speech.

_____ 4. In the last two national elections the majority of the people voted in favor of the conservative Republican Party. This fact suggests that Americans are generally becoming more conservative.

_____ 5. A random sampling of one-fourth of the student population revealed that over 70% are interested in more funding for instruction and less for sports. Our student body is apparently more interested in receiving a good education than in sponsoring a good sports program.

_____ 6. Although most of the studies conclude that eighteen year olds are more likely to be involved in drinking and driving accidents than any other population group, it seems clear to me that teenagers are some of the most responsible and safest drivers on the road.

_____ 7. A study of Australian sheep farmers indicated that most have killed wild rabbits that damage their land. It seems clear that American farmers also have little respect for wildlife and are bent on pushing the bald eagle into extinction.

_____ 8. The recent government reductions in spending are forcing the elderly of this country to go without food. The city of New York reported finding six elderly street people who appeared significantly undernourished.

_____ 9. With half of the people of this city opposed to an increase in taxes, it seems clear that the mandate favors no increase for this year.

_____ 10. Informal comments from local officials and a recent opinion offered by the chief of police make it clear that our city is safer now than it was ten years ago.

Name______________________________ Date______________ Score__________

ACTIVITY 44-2, EFFECTIVE EVIDENCE

Choose the best among the following evidence offered in support of the stated opinion, placing an E before each item of sound evidence. Place an X before each piece of evidence which you would not use. Below the rejected evidence state the reason for your rejection.

Opinion: A knowledge of computers is becoming essential in the modern business world.

Evidence:

______ 1. Nine out of ten businesses make use of computers.

______ 2. The largest job demand in the business fields is related to computer use and repair.

______ 3. Most computer service students are friendly.

______ 4. The opinion of a respected professional athlete, however, is that the computer fad is short term.

______ 5. Most new secretarial positions require a basic understanding of computer processing.

______ 6. My mother, who was an executive secretary before she retired, states, however, that all a good secretary needs is a stenographer's pad and a typewriter.

______ 7. Older business executives are now taking five-week courses in computer use.

______ 8. Computer science is becoming the most popular course of twenty-year-old female students.

______ 9. The majority opinion among public school teachers is that computers will cause more problems for business than they will solve.

______ 10. My best friend, who took six courses in computer science before dropping out of college, is now unemployed.

______ 11. Related to the importance of computers in the business setting, a random sampling N = 1047 with T-value of .79 indicated a positive correlation with statistical significance at the .01 level.

______ 12. A study conducted during the '70's by a major business magazine indicated that most computers would be too cumbersome for office use.

Name______________________________ Date______________ Score_________

ACTIVITY 45-1, VALID ARGUMENTS

The following sentences make use of either valid or invalid reasoning. Place an L before those statements which are logical and an F before those sentences which use faulty logic.

1. Anyone who has bought a new car knows that the American auto industry is in trouble.

2. If the quality of American products improves, those customers who are concerned with quality will give more consideration to American products.

3. Pollution affects people emotionally as well as physically. Since the building of two new factories in the '70's, the divorce rate in our town has increased significantly.

4. No thinking person can favor both business and the worker.

5. Japanese televisions are superior to American sets because the Japanese worker doesn't have the stress caused by mandatory social security contributions.

6. Many people will buy the least expensive product. Since many imported products are less expensive than American products, these people tend to buy imports.

7. America was a good place to live and work before the government established so many pollution laws.

8. Organized crime is involved in pollution; as soon as pollution laws were established, there were any number of violators.

9. Nine out of ten who were fired by one major manufacturer stated that they thought the company was unfair to its workers.

10. American products are durable and inexpensive because they last a long time and they cost little.

11. The best reason to buy Japanese cars is that throughout the Orient there are young people who simply want a better job and a better way of life.

12. This year's record high sales of American-made automobiles will probably help American industry.

13. As a rule, big business is greedy. The evidence is everywhere in the cost of products.

14. Several workers in a Las Vegas shoe factory support my view that their industry has almost been driven under by the popular summer habit of not wearing shoes to the beach.

15. Americans are world leaders in high technology. As a consequence, we should also be respected as the finest craftsmen of custom-made silverware.

16. Either we must stop buying all foreign goods by the end of this year or our children and children's children will be unemployed.

17. Middle class workers will continue to buy imported goods, but they never seem to know what's important.

18. Any time that one speaks of quality products in a competitive industry, one should consider our educational opportunities, which, in America, are second to none.

19. Industry is the most important income provider in those areas in which it provides a major portion of the salaries.

20. If this country were ever to lose its major industries, it is likely that many of those people employed by industry would be at least temporarily out of work.

Name______________________________ Date______________ Score_________

ACTIVITY 45-2, VALID ARGUMENTS

The third statement in each of the groups below represents a conclusion based on the previous two statements. If the conclusion is reasonable, underline it. If it is not reasonable, then offer a substitute conclusion, or indicate that no logical conclusion can be drawn.

1. Of a random sampling of 500 wealthy business executives, 400 indicated that they were Republicans.

   Of a similar sampling of 500 laborers, 473 indicated that they were Democrats.

   The Republican party seems to be more popular among those who have above-average incomes.

____

____

2. Under the new superintendent the city transportation has provided better services during the past year and has actually decreased its cost.

   Recent investigations have revealed that the superintendent of transportation has relatives belonging to the Ku Klux Klan.

   The superintendent should therefore be fired.

____

____

3. My art teacher, who is from Poland, is a very sickly person.

   My mother's friend from Honduras has high blood pressure.

   Most foreign nations have poor health services.

____

____

4. Most South Americans speak either Spanish or Portuguese.

   Jose has just moved to the U.S. from Brazil.

   Odds are that he speaks either Spanish or Portuguese.

____

____

5. I made my best grade in mathematics the day after I took a large dose of vitamin C.

   I have been taking vitamin C every day for a month.

   It seems certain that I will make a good grade on my next mathematics test.

____

____

6. For the last ten years the speed limit has been 55 miles per hour.

   During this period, there have been fewer accidents and fewer automobile related deaths than during earlier times when the speed limit was higher.

   Certainly, we can raise the speed limit now that people know how to drive safely.

____

____

7. Everyone agrees that the American way is being threatened by foreign investors.

   And we all know the foreign investors build unsafe plants.

   Therefore, patriotic Americans should not work for anyone with a foreign background.

____

____

8. Recent studies suggest that men who smoke greatly increase their chances of cancer and heart problems.

Studies also indicate that women who smoke have a higher incidence of serious health problems.

It seems evident that only younger women should smoke.

____

____

9. Most college professors are bleeding-heart liberals.

The majority of them have no backbone.

Thus, a student can rest assured that he will get an A in a course, no matter how poorly he performs.

____

____

10. The mothers of the members of the gang stated that their children are good people.

The fathers stated that their children never did anything for which they were punished.

Based on their statements, it seems clear that the police have accused innocent people.

____

____